DESIRE FOR CONTROL

PERSONALITY, SOCIAL, AND CLINICAL PERSPECTIVES

THE PLENUM SERIES IN SOCIAL / CLINICAL PSYCHOLOGY

Series Editor: C. R. Snyder

University of Kansas
Lawrence, Kansas

A Continuation Order Plan is available for this series. A continuation order will bring delivery of each new volume immediately upon publication. Volumes are billed only upon actual shipment. For further information please contact the publisher.

DESIRE FOR CONTROL

PERSONALITY, SOCIAL, AND CLINICAL PERSPECTIVES

JERRY M. BURGER

Santa Clara University
Santa Clara, California

PLENUM PRESS • NEW YORK AND LONDON

Library of Congress Cataloging-in-Publication Data

Burger, Jerry M.
    Desire for control : personality, social, and clinical
perspectives / Jerry M. Burger.
        p.   cm. -- (The Plenum series in social/clinical psychology)
    Includes bibliographical references and index.
    ISBN 0-306-44072-5
    1. Control (Psychology)   I. Title. II. Series.
    [DNLM: 1. Personality Assessment. 2. Power (Psychology)   WM
460.5M6 B954d]
    BF611.B87 1992
    155.2--dc20
DNLM/DLC
for Library of Congress   92-3423
                                                               CIP

ISBN 0-306-44072-5

© 1992 Plenum Press, New York
A Division of Plenum Publishing Corporation
233 Spring Street, New York, N.Y. 10013

Printed in the United States of America

To Adam

PREFACE

This book is a cumulation of a research program that began in the summer of 1978, when I was a doctoral student at the University of Missouri. What started as a graduate student's curiosity about individual differences in need for personal control led to a personality scale, a few publications, some additional questions, and additional research. For reasons I no longer recall, I named this personality trait *desire for control*. One study led to another, and questions by students and colleagues often spurred me to apply desire for control to new areas and new questions.

At the same time, researchers around the globe began using the scale and sending me reprints of articles and copies of papers describing work they had done on desire for control. In the past decade or so, I have talked or corresponded with dozens of students who have used the scale in their doctoral dissertation and master's thesis research. I have heard of or seen translations of the Desirability of Control Scale into German, Polish, Japanese, and French. There is also a children's version of the scale. I estimate that there have now been more than a hundred studies conducted on desire for control.

One problem with this research is that it has often been developed in a topic-by-topic fashion, with each new experiment tied loosely to a few others. The result has been a scattering of information about desire for control throughout journals and conferences. Moreover, many studies, including quite a few of my own, have not been published. I have copies of many of these unpublished studies, but almost no one else knows about them. Consequently, one reason for writing this book was to bring together all this research into one comprehensive package that provides a more complete picture of what we know about desire for control. My hope is that the book will stimulate even more interest in desire for control and will be of great help to researchers hoping to build on others' work with this personality variable.

I maintain throughout the book that desire for control is a general personality trait with relevance to a large number of behaviors of interest to psychologists. I have been particularly struck by the importance of desire for control in understanding many topics of interest to both social psychologists and clinical psychologists. As this series of books attests, the past decade has seen a growing awareness among psychologists of various stripes of the relationship between social psychology and clinical psychology. It is my belief that desire for control represents one of the many bridges between these two fields. As will be seen, research demonstrates that individual differences in desire for control affect both social behavior and traditional clinical phenomena. Understanding a person's behavior in one of these areas provides a better understanding of behavior in the other. Consequently, a second reason for writing this book was to illustrate how desire for control helps to tie social and clinical phenomena together.

ACKNOWLEDGMENTS

Of course, no program of research is conducted alone, even when the researcher suffers from an excessively high desire for control. I would like to thank Harris Cooper and Bob Arkin, who gave me encouragement and advice (and just a little bit of grief) at the beginning of this process and who served as coauthors on the first desire for control papers. This is also the time to acknowledge the contribution of all the other colleagues and students who coauthored papers. The list includes Garrell Bullard, Linda Burns, Chris Crowe, Tim Hemans, Randy Husbands, Dennis LaTorre, Jenny McWard, Julie Oakman, Mike Santos, Deb Schnerring, Marlan Schwartz, Norris Smith, Cecilia Solano, Bob Vartabedian, Mark Wilsmann, and Larry Young. Beyond this, there are the dozens of students who served as research assistants, all of whom I thank once again. I also want to express my appreciation for the support and encouragement I received from Marlene, who has been with me throughout this process. Finally, this book is dedicated to Adam, with the hope that you learn to express your own desire for control well as I learn to grant you the personal control you need.

Jerry M. Burger

Santa Clara, California

CONTENTS

Chapter 6

Attributions and Information Processing 101

Chapter 7

Well-Being, Adjustment, and Health 119

CHAPTER 1

INTRODUCTION

The seed for the research reported in this book was planted nearly two decades ago. Like a lot of students attending college in California in the early 1970s, I found myself participating in an encounter group with about a dozen other students. In the middle of our fourth or fifth session, I remember asking myself this question: "Why am I hating this?" The answer came to me after a little reflection—I hate this because what happens during the two hours I spend twice a week in this windowless room is almost totally out of my control. The rules for social interaction I used to control my daily conversations did not apply here. Group members were encouraged to speak their minds and do whatever they wanted. The sessions seemed chaotic, and my attempts to establish some order or direction to our activities were either rejected or simply ignored.

I shared this insight with a few group members outside of our sessions and with other people I knew who were trying out similar encounter group experiences. Some knew exactly what I was talking about, but others did not understand the problem. I learned from these and other conversations that I seemed to have a much higher need to control what happens to me than most of my friends. Following this insight, evidence for my high need for control began popping up everywhere. I became very upset when, despite my planning, some friends and I got lost in San Francisco. Not knowing where I was or how to get where I wanted to go was a real problem for me. My friends just took it in stride. After I had peppered my physician with a dozen or more questions during an office visit, he remarked that most of his patients were content to let him make the decisions and did not need all this information about what he was doing and why. Whenever an instructor assigned group projects for a class, I found myself taking charge and

1

doing most of the work. When a fellow student asked me one day why I did not spread the work around a little more, I explained that I needed to be sure that the project went the way I wanted it to.

These observations about my high need for control led to an interest in research on personal control in graduate school and, as I describe in the next chapter, eventually to my own research on individual differences in this need. The outgrowth has been more than a dozen years of research by me and others on what I began calling the *desire for control*. This book was designed to bring together all of this research in an effort to paint a comprehensive picture of this personality variable. In addition, this book was organized to illustrate that individual differences in desire for control play an important role in many social and clinical phenomena. But before describing more precisely what I mean by desire for control, it is useful to understand how the concept of personal control fits within current and past psychological research and theory.

PERSONAL CONTROL IN PSYCHOLOGY RESEARCH

The notion of personal control has played a central role in a large amount of psychological research over the past few decades. Topics that touch on the issues of perceived or desired control include learned helplessness, the Type A Behavior Pattern, intrinsic motivation, social influence, need for power, locus of control, predictability, and others. I once did a quick, informal survey of articles appearing in the personality processes and individual difference section of the *Journal of Personality and Social Psychology* over a seven-year period in the mid 1980s. I counted the number of articles that I felt dealt with personal control issues. Although admittedly fairly subjective, my coding system also seemed to me to be appropriately restrictive. I found that slightly more than three out of four monthly issues of the journal contained at least one article about personal control. In total, 13.7% (almost one in seven) fell into this category. I interpret these data to mean that personal control has become one of the central concepts in recent personality research.

The extent to which people perceive or prefer control has also become increasingly relevant for psychologists working in other subfields of the discipline, in particular social psychology and clinical psychology. Researchers often use personal control to explain behaviors in such traditional social psychology areas as achievement motivation, crowding, attribution theory, leadership, education, aggression, and interpersonal relationships. Similarly, clinical topics such as depression, coping with stress, anorexia and bulimia, alcohol and drug abuse, and problem gambling have been examined in terms of the extent to which people want and see themselves in control of relevant events.

As described in the next section, many theorists and researchers have argued that, all things being equal, each of us prefers to exercise some control over what happens to us. We usually want to make our own decisions, act in our own behalf, and take responsibility for making what we will of our lives. For many years it seemed that perceived control was a panacea for many of the problems psychologists studied. For example, feeling that one was in control was said to increase performance on achievement tasks (Perlmuter & Monty, 1977) while a perception that one has lost control was tied to increased susceptibility to depression (Seligman, 1975).

More recently, researchers have recognized that people do not always prefer to control the situations they encounter (Burger, 1989a; Folkman, 1984; Rodin, Rennert, & Solomon, 1980; Thompson, Cheek, & Graham, 1987). For example, increased control often means increased responsibility and increased pressure to perform well. While sometimes this pressure can lead to a better performance, sometimes it does not (Burger, 1987b). Thus, while a promotion and increased responsibility may be desirable in many ways, these come with added problems and dangers. An increase in personal control might also mean that one is less likely to obtain desired outcomes. For example, I might not want to take control of a group project when other group members could do a better job that will ultimately benefit me more. Sometimes we prefer to give others control over situations with potentially serious consequences if we believe those other people are better able to avoid negative outcomes (Burger, McWard, & LaTorre, 1989). Thus, people sometimes give up their car keys rather than retaining personal control over getting home when they have had too much to drink.

In short, although many psychologists have made the case that, all things being equal, people generally prefer to have some ability to control what happens to them, all things are rarely equal. Despite the panacea-like terms with which many psychologists once described personal control, therapists should not always strive to provide their clients with more control over stressful events (Brehm & Smith, 1986), and health practitioners should not assume that patients prefer to control medical decisions and procedures as much as possible (Reid, 1984). In any given situation, many variables affect whether a person prefers control and will respond well if given it. One of the key variables in this process is how much that person generally likes to feel in control of events. As the research in this book demonstrates, some people prefer to control the events in their lives more than others.

MOTIVATION FOR CONTROL
IN PERSONALITY PSYCHOLOGY

The notion that people prefer to control the events in their lives can be found in many different forms throughout writings and research by personality psychologists. Among the first to discuss this concept was Alfred Adler, who identified what he called a *striving for superiority* as the primary human motive (Adler, 1930; Ansbacher & Ansbacher, 1956). According to Adler, each child perceives his or her inferiority to the stronger and more capable people he or she encounters. "To be human means to feel inferior," Adler wrote. Most people are said to respond to this perception with a lifelong effort to overcome these feelings of inferiority and to demonstrate their superiority. Thus, people work hard at their jobs, get involved in political and social movements, and compete in sports and games to demonstrate to themselves and others that they are masterful, achieving people and not the inferior beings they were in childhood.

Adler's description of superiority striving has many similarities to later theories that emphasize the importance of demonstrating one's ability to control or master life's challenges. However, it is never clear from reading Adler's words whether achieving this control is satisfying in itself or whether it primarily serves the function of momentarily alleviating the feelings of inferiority that haunt us. It is not clear whether people ever obtain a sense of personal satisfaction from a job well done or a difficult obstacle overcome. Instead, one gets a picture of a runner trapped a few steps behind an elusive image of success while desperately trying to stay ahead of a relentless image of failure.

The first comprehensive description of a motive to exercise control for its own sake was presented by Robert White (1959). White proposed that many human behaviors could be best understood in terms of what he identified as *competence* or *effectance* motivation. He argued that young children do not explore and manipulate objects because this behavior satisfies some primary need, but rather because the behavior "satisfies an intrinsic need to deal with the environment." Similarly, adults can spend endless hours trying to master challenges at work or even building a model ship as a hobby. They do these things not because they seek the external rewards that come with the accomplishment, but rather to obtain a sense of mastery over their environment.

White acknowledged that competence motivation was but one of many motives, and that often more primary needs will take precedence in determining behavior. However, he also emphasized that much of what is interpreted as an effort to obtain external rewards is, in fact, motivated by a need to see oneself as a competent and masterful person. "Effectance motivation is persistent," White wrote. "It regularly occupies the spare waking time between episodes of homeostatic crisis" (p. 322). Thus, unlike Adler, White maintained that exercising control over the obstacles and challenges in one's environment is satisfying in its own right. A woman might work on the crossword puzzle every morning not because she seeks reinforcement from others, but because completing the puzzle provides a "feeling of efficacy."

This idea was developed even further by Richard deCharms (1968). DeCharms argued that the person we typically describe as high in need for achievement is someone who derives a sense of "intrinsic satisfaction" from competition with others or comparison with a standard of achievement. Like many motives identified and explored by researchers, achievement motivation can be conceived of in terms of a larger motivation construct. DeCharms identified this larger construct as "the desire to be master of one's fate." Thus, deCharms appears to be describing a motivation to exercise effective control over what happens to us. "Man strives to be a causal agent," he wrote. "To be the primary locus of causation for, or the origin of, his behavior; he strives for personal causation" (p. 269). According to this viewpoint, exercising control is more than satisfying in itself. The need to control one's world underlies many of the behaviors and motives examined by psychologists.

The notion that people are motivated to feel like masterful and effective agents capable of influencing the events in their environment was also promoted by Ed Deci (1975) and others who drew a distinction between extrinsic and intrinsic sources of motivation. Extrinsically motivated behaviors are those engaged in to obtain rewards from others, such as working for money. We engage in intrinsically motivated behavior to satisfy internal sources of gratification. Deci (1975) originally described these internal sources of motivation in terms of demonstrating one's mastery and competence. Like White and deCharms, he argued that people work on tasks not only because they might receive some sort of payment or interpersonal gain, but many times because they want to demonstrate to themselves that they are capable of effectively exercising control over their environments.

In later writings Deci and his colleagues drew a distinction between control and what they termed *self-determination* (Deci, 1980; Deci & Ryan, 1985b). They argued that people may not always prefer to control what happens to them. Rather, they are motivated to maintain a sense of choice over what happens to them; that is, their behavior is self-determined. Deci provides the example of someone who chooses to ride in the pas-

senger seat rather than drive a car. This person has more or less relin-
quished control over the movement of the car, but has maintained a
sense of self-determination because he or she is doing what he or she
wanted. As described later, the way Deci and his colleagues describe the
term *self-determination* is very similar to the way I use the term *control*.

Finally, Albert Bandura (1977, 1986) has promoted a concept he
labels *self-efficacy*. According to this approach, we can understand behavior change by examining the extent to which people expect that they are
capable of performing the behaviors required to reach their goals. That
is, how strongly we believe we can control events determines how much
effort we put into change and how long these efforts persist. Bandura
(1977) draws a distinction between self-efficacy and White's effectance
motivation, painting self-efficacy in cognitive rather than drive terms.
According to Bandura, it is the expectation of personal control that underlies the motivation behind many behaviors, rather than a need to
demonstrate mastery.

In summary, many psychologists have identified a motivation for
personal control or a similar concept in their work. Although only a few
of the more prominent theories were touched on here, the point is that
in one way or another a number of psychologists have recognized or
acknowledged that people often are motivated to control the events in
their environment and that this motivation plays an important role in
human behavior.

INDIVIDUAL DIFFERENCES IN DESIRE FOR CONTROL

Although people may be motivated to exercise control over many
of the events in their lives, observation should tell us that this motive is
not present to the same extent in all people. We all know someone who
is highly motivated to make the decisions in a relationship, take on the
leadership role in a group, and to demonstrate his or her ability to
conquer any and all challenging tasks. On the other hand, we all have
also encountered someone who shows little of these inclinations and who
seems more than willing to allow others to make decisions and take
responsibility for group activities. The remainder of this book is devoted
to exploring these individual differences in desire for control.

Desire for control is defined as the extent to which people generally
are motivated to see themselves in control of the events in their lives. I
conceive of desire for control as a personality trait. Like other trait variables, each of us can be placed somewhere along a continuum ranging
from those with an extremely low desire for control to those with an

extremely high desire for control. Although the people who fall at the ends of the continuum are the most interesting, most of us fall somewhere in the middle. Naturally, each of us experiences situations in which we prefer to exercise a great deal of control, just as each of us can think of situations over which we would just as soon have little or no control. However, as with other personality traits, there is a general level of desire for control that theoretically can be determined with enough observations of a person's behavior over a significant amount of time and in many different situations.

All of the research reported in this book operationally defines *desire for control* in terms of the score people obtain on the Desirability of Control Scale, as described in the next chapter. However, before turning to a description of the scale and its psychometric properties, a few conceptual issues need to be addressed. In particular, I conceive of desire for control as a general personality trait, as opposed to a domain-specific construct. Further, I think of control in terms of direct actions or choices, rather than indirect means of dealing with a need for control.

DESIRE FOR CONTROL AS A GENERAL PERSONALITY TRAIT

There has been a growing trend in personality research over the past decade or so to increase the predictive power of personality trait measures by assessing a narrower or more domain-specific aspect of the trait. For example, we can do a better job of predicting social behavior by using a measure of sociability, one of the components that make up the more general trait of extraversion, than by looking at a measure of extraversion (Wolfe & Kasmer, 1988). Similarly, looking at locus of control scores for specific domains, such as marriage or academic achievement, predicts marriage and academic behaviors better than using a general locus of control score.

However, the work reported in this book has thus far managed to avoid the temptation to narrow the scope of the desire for control construct. Instead, I prefer to think of desire for control in very general terms. That is, I maintain that we can identify a general level of desire for control that is related to behavior and experiences over many different aspects of a person's life. People who generally prefer to control what happens to them at work also tend to want to control what happens to them in their interpersonal relations. If someone typically does not like to take on leadership positions in group settings, that person probably also does not want to exercise a great amount of control over his or her health care. Indeed, as the table of contents for this book illustrates, other researchers and I have had great success at using a general desire for control score to predict behavior in a wide variety of situations.

Of course, it certainly is possible to develop desire for control measures for specific experiences in people's lives. For example, scales developed to measure desire for control over health care do a better job of predicting health care behaviors than a measure of general desire for control (Smith, Wallston, Wallston, Forsberg, & King, 1984). But I am arguing that each of these domain-specific measures of desire for control is really assessing a part of a larger, more general personality variable. In addition to addressing the specific issues identified in each chapter, the research reviewed in this book gives us an idea of the scope of this broad personality construct.

PRIMARY VERSUS SECONDARY CONTROL

Some researchers have drawn a distinction between what is sometimes called *primary control* and *secondary control* (cf. Rothbaum, Weisz, & Snyder, 1982). *Primary control* generally refers to direct efforts to change the environment, whereas Rothbaum *et al.* describe *secondary control* in terms of people "bringing themselves into line with environmental forces" so as to avoid the perception that they are out of control. Examples of secondary control use include people who rely on superstitious behavior to obtain desired outcomes and people who align themselves with powerful others to vicariously share the feelings of power and control. Although the link between what are identified as primary and secondary efforts at maintaining control remains an interesting question, the research on desire for control reported here is based on a definition of control in terms of direct actions and choices rather than the use of secondary control tactics. One might say that the Desirability of Control Scale is designed to measure motivation to engage in primary control rather than rely on secondary control procedures. Indeed, as discussed in later chapters, research finds that desire for control people are not as likely as people with a low desire for control to use superstitious behavior or relinquish control to more powerful others.

SUMMARY

The concept of *personal control* can be found throughout research in personality, social psychology, and clinical psychology. Although much early research suggested that the more control one has over any given event the better, more recent work has identified many exceptions to this rule. Nonetheless, all things being equal, people probably prefer exercising control over not exercising control.

This book is concerned with the extent to which people generally are motivated to see themselves in control of the events in their lives. Similar constructs have been introduced and developed by personality psychologists for many decades. The work on desire for control should not be thought of as unrelated to this earlier theorizing, nor should it simply be seen as building on past theories. Rather, I prefer to think of the research described in this book as a different way to examine a recurring theme in the study of human behavior, namely the motivation to exercise personal control. My colleagues and I have looked at this motivation from an individual differences perspective, arguing that people differ in the extent to which they typically prefer to see themselves in control. As such, research into desire for control should be seen as a complement to this earlier work.

I have resisted the temptation to narrow the focus of desire for control to specific behavior domains. Rather, I have tried to do just the opposite—to show that desire for control can be thought of as a very general trait relevant to a wide range of behaviors. In any given situation, the extent to which a person wants to control what happens would seem to be a crucial piece of information for predicting his or her behavior. If we can identify a person's general level of desire for control, then we should better understand what he or she does in many parts of his or her life.

CHAPTER 2

MEASURING
DESIRE FOR CONTROL

In the summer of 1978, while driving north on Interstate 99 just past Bakersfield, it dawned on me that the topics in psychology that interested me the most at the time—learned helplessness, attributions, social influence, and others—all had something to do with the issue of personal control. Because I had often reflected on my own high need for control, I speculated about the role this individual difference variable might play in many of these areas. Before reaching Fresno I had definite plans to investigate individual differences in the extent to which people prefer to control the events in their lives. I was quite eager to begin searching through the available personality scales and decide which of the need for control tests best matched the construct as I conceptualized it and would best meet my research needs.

Unfortunately, many hours of looking through endless journals and books only left me empty handed. I found several scales designed to measure similar constructs, but nothing specifically developed to measure a general need to feel in control of the events in one's life. And so I proposed to a colleague, Harris Cooper, that I develop my own scale. He reluctantly agreed to help me with this project. The Desirability of Control Scale emerged from that endeavor, and with it the beginning of more than a decade of fruitful research.

The research reviewed in this book is concerned with the desire for control construct as measured by the Desirability of Control (DC) Scale. Although many related personality scales have been developed and used to explore many of the topics dealt with here, I have chosen to limit the scope of this book to research using the DC Scale. This

11

approach has several advantages. The most important of these advantages is that comparison across studies is much easier when the major
independent variable is operationalized in an identical manner. Interpreting and reconciling inconsistent research findings is often impossible
when researchers use different scales to measure the same variable. In
these cases it is difficult to know if the inconsistencies might not be due
simply to the fact that the different tests do not quite measure the same
thing. Nowhere is this problem more apparent today than in the Type
A Behavior Pattern literature, in which different relationships between
Type A personality and health can be found depending on how Type A
personality is measured (Matthews & Haynes, 1986).

Another reason to limit the discussion to research using the DC
Scale is that it allows me to present a comprehensive picture of work in
this area, which would be impossible if I tried to cover all the research
conducted with related or similar personality scales. The DC Scale is not
the only way to measure individual differences in need for control, but
no other scale measuring a motivation for (as contrasted with a perception of) personal control has generated as much research. In addition, I
know of no other scale that was developed specifically to measure a
general need for control. Some scales have been constructed to measure
control over a specific type of situation, such as health care or relationships. And some scales measure constructs that are theoretically related
to a need for control, such as Type A behavior scales and need for
achievement measures. But none of these instruments captures the construct as I originally conceptualized it.

I developed the Desirability of Control Scale with Harris Cooper in
1978 and published the scale the following year. Somewhere in the process we began using the term *desire for control* instead of need for control,
but the reasons for this choice elude me today. A detailed presentation
of the scale development process and the associated psychometric data
can be found in the original article (Burger & Cooper, 1979). I will briefly
describe that process below, as well as the scale's relationship with other
personality trait measures.

SCALE DEVELOPMENT

We began the process of developing a scale to measure individual
differences in a general need for control by generating self-descriptive
statements that we believed captured the personality construct we were
interested in assessing. We tried to think of some general statements (for
example, "I enjoy making my own decisions") as well as statements that

described specific situations for which we guessed desire for control would play a role (for example "I am careful to check everything on an automobile before I leave for a long trip"). To avoid the problem of an acquiescence response (Nunnally, 1967), items were written so that sometimes agreeing with the statement indicated a low desire for control. Fifty-three statements were generated through this process.

The 53 items were administered to a large undergraduate sample. The 453 students in the sample were asked to indicate on seven-point scales the extent to which each of the statements applied to them. Next, using a procedure outlined by Nunnally (1967), we systematically dropped the items with the lowest overall correlation with the total score until we obtained the group of items with the highest internal consistency. We also checked the standard deviations of these items to assure that each had an adequate range of possible responses. The 20 items that emerged from this process constituted the Desirability of Control Scale. The scale is shown in Figure 1.

RELIABILITY OF THE DC SCALE

One essential feature for a useful personality inventory is that it measure whatever it measures consistently, that is, the scale's reliability. Data relevant to assessing the reliability of the DC Scale address two questions. First, do all the test items hang together, or appear to be measuring the same construct? This is the question of internal consistency. Next, are scale scores consistent over time? In both cases, the available evidence indicates that the DC Scale is quite reliable.

INTERNAL CONSISTENCY

Naturally, we examined indices of internal consistency during the test construction. We computed a Kuder–Richardson 20 internal consistency coefficient of .80 in the original sample. Although this level of reliability is well within the acceptable range for this type of personality scale, we had to recognize that the procedure used to select the final 20 items from the original pool of items capitalized on chance. That is, the 20 items were selected precisely because they generated a high internal consistency coefficient with this sample, but might not with another sample. Therefore, we administered the scale to a second undergraduate sample and, to our surprise, a Kuder–Richardson 20 coefficient of .81 emerged from our analysis of this second sample. Thus, we were satisfied that the scale items all seemed to be measuring the same general construct.

Below you will find a series of statements. Please read each statement carefully and respond to it by expressing the extent to which you believe the statement applies to you. For all items, a response from 1 to 7 is required. Use the number that best reflects your belief when the scale is defined as follows:

1 = The statement does not apply to me at all
2 = The statement usually does not apply to me
3 = Most often, the statement does not apply
4 = I am unsure about whether or not the statement
 applies to me, or it applies to me about half the time
5 = The statement applies more often than not
6 = The statement usually applies to me
7 = The statement always applies to me

_____ 1. I prefer a job where I have a lot of control over what I do and when I do it.
_____ 2. I enjoy political participation because I want to have as much of a say in running government as possible.
_____ 3. I try to avoid situations where someone else tells me what to do.
_____ 4. I would prefer to be a leader than a follower.
_____ 5. I enjoy being able to influence the actions of others.
_____ 6. I am careful to check everything on an automobile before I leave for a long trip.
_____ 7. Others usually know what is best for me.
_____ 8. I enjoy making my own decisions.
_____ 9. I enjoy having control over my own destiny.
_____ 10. I would rather someone else take over the leadership role when I'm involved in a group project.
_____ 11. I consider myself to be generally more capable of handling situations than others are.
_____ 12. I'd rather run my own business and make my own mistakes than listen to someone else's orders.
_____ 13. I like to get a good idea of what a job is all about before I begin.
_____ 14. When I see a problem, I prefer to do something about it rather than sit by and let it continue.
_____ 15. When it comes to orders, I would rather give them than receive them.
_____ 16. I wish I could push many of life's daily decisions off on someone else.
_____ 17. When driving, I try to avoid putting myself in a situation where I could be hurt by another person's mistake.
_____ 18. I prefer to avoid situations where someone else has to tell me what it is I should be doing.
_____ 19. There are many situations in which I would prefer only one choice rather than having to make a decision.
_____ 20. I like to wait and see if someone else is going to solve a problem so that I don't have to be bothered with it.

To score, reverse the values of the answers to items 7, 10, 16, 19, and 20 (that is, 1 = 7, 2 = 6, and so on). Then add the twenty answer values together. Means for the scale from various samples tend to come out around 100, with a standard deviation of about 10.

FIGURE 1. The Desirability of Control Scale

Several additional investigators have also reported internal consistency data for the DC Scale when administering the scale to samples from diverse populations. The data from these studies tend to be in line with those reported with our original samples. For example, Smith *et al.* (1984) administered the DC Scale to three varied samples of adults: women visiting obstetricians, people seeking information about dying and bereavement, and people attending church or waiting in a university medical center. The investigators report alpha reliability coefficients of .74, .81, and .78, respectively, for these samples. Ryland and Levy (1988) administered the DC Scale to a large sample of employees in financial aid offices. They calculated an alpha coefficient of .78 for the scale. Reed (1989) reports a Cronbach's alpha coefficient of .77 with a sample of union organizers.

Other evidence for the internal consistency of the scale comes from Braukmann (1981), who translated the DC Scale into German, but modified the response options from seven-point to five-point scales. Nonetheless, he computed a Cronbach alpha of .77 for the translated scale and a Spearman–Brown coefficient of .76. In short, data from a number of different populations suggest that the DC Scale possesses adequate internal consistency.

(

TEST–RETEST RELIABILITY

Another important test of reliability concerns the consistency of scale scores over time. If, as we suggest, a person's level of desire for control is relatively stable over time, then we should find reasonably high correlations between test scores when the scale is given to the same sample after a short time span. Unfortunately, because researchers are rarely interested in administering the same personality scale to people on more than one occasion, information about the stability of desire for control scores over time is limited. In our original sample, we found a test–retest correlation of .75 over a six-week period (Burger & Cooper, 1979). I unintentionally obtained some test–retest data in another investigation when I administered the DC Scale to some undergraduate students at the beginning of the semester and at the end of the semester (Burger, 1980). Although the sample size was small, I found a correlation of .69 with a 12- to 14-week interval between tests. Much stronger evidence for the scale's test–retest reliability was reported by Braukmann (1981) with the German version of the DC Scale. He administered the test to a large sample ($N = 162$) of subjects one year after the initial testing and found a correlation of .70 between the two test scores. In summary, there is good evidence that DC Scale scores remain stable over reasonable periods of time.

But the most intriguing data on this question come from a 10-year follow-up study I conducted recently with a colleague at Wake Forest University (Burger & Solano, 1991). Through a mail survey, we administered the DC Scale in the fall of 1990 to 135 people who had completed the scale as undergraduates at Wake Forest in the fall of 1980. We found a correlation of .63 between the two sets of scores for the male subjects. However, we found a correlation of only .11 between 1980 and 1990 DC Scale scores for the female subjects. The changes in the women's desire for control levels will be addressed later in this chapter.

FACTOR ANALYSES

Although we were interested in developing a scale to measure a unidimensional construct, we also recognized that the items we used to measure this construct might be divided into smaller components. Therefore, we conducted a factor analysis of the data from our original sample. We identified five factors in this analysis accounting for slightly more than 50% of the original scale variation. An examination of the five factors, in order of size, suggested the following general categories: a General Desire for Control factor (for example, "I enjoy having control over my own destiny"); a Decisiveness factor (for example, "There are many situations in which I would prefer only one choice rather than having to make a decision"); a Preparation–Prevention Control factor (for example, "I like to get a good idea of what a job is all about before I begin"); an Avoidance of Dependence factor (for example, "I try to avoid situations where someone else tells me what to do"); and a Leadership factor (for example, "I would rather someone else take over the leadership role when I'm involved in a group project").

Other factor analyses have produced slightly different results. We conducted a second factor analysis with another sample and produced a similar, but not identical, pattern of factors to the five described above (Burger & Cooper, 1979). Similarly, Kluger (1988) reports a factor analysis of the scale that produced five nearly identical factors to those we found in our original sample. Braukmann (1981) factor analyzed the items on his German version of the DC Scale. He also generated five factors in this analysis, but the loadings were different from those in our research. Braukmann's first three factors appear to deal with influence over others, relinquishing control to others, and making decisions. The last two factors are much less easy to interpret. Using his own German version of the DC Scale, Schönbach (1990) generated only two factors. One of these contained items generally concerned with what Schönbach called the *need for competence and influence*. The other factor he labeled the *need for constancy and shielding*. The distinction he draws appears to be essentially the difference between a need to exercise control over the environment and a need to have a predictable environment that does not exert a high level of influence on us.

In short, although not always producing identical results, factor analyses of the 20 scale items have succeeded in identifying components of the scale that make some intuitive sense. Because we are necessarily limited to the items on this or any other scale to measure the construct, it is not surprising that factors identified with such labels as *decisiveness* and *leadership* surface in these factor analyses. We included these items in the original pool because we felt that decisiveness and leadership were characteristic of people with a high desire for control. Although examining one or more of these components may make sense in a particular investigation, the internal consistency data indicate that we also are justified in treating the overall desire for control score as a unidimensional construct. From the beginning we have conceived of desire for control as a general construct that surfaces in many types of situations, such as when making decisions and when in a situation that requires some leadership.

VALIDITY OF THE DC SCALE

Perhaps the most difficult task in test construction is demonstrating that the instrument measures what it is designed to measure, in other words, establishing evidence for the validity of the test. We now have a great deal of research demonstrating that people who score high on the DC Scale tend to behave differently than those who score low in ways that indicate their generally higher need to control the events in their lives. This research is reviewed throughout this book.

Test makers also should provide evidence for the test's discriminant validity. That is, we need to demonstrate that the DC Scale does not correlate highly with scales measuring conceptually different constructs. On the other hand, particularly because we conceive of desire for control as a general personality variable, we should expect DC Scale scores to be moderately related to many other personality traits. Evidence for these moderate correlations, known as convergent validity, helps us understand the nomological network in which the desire for control construct is embedded.

The notion of personal control has become quite popular in psychology research in the past two decades. Consequently, a large number of personality scales have been developed to measure various kinds of perceived control, motivation for control, and concepts that seem to be similar or at least related to what I am calling desire for control. A large number of investigations from many different researchers now provide a picture of how desire for control fits with these other personality dimensions. This research is reviewed in the next section.

LOCUS OF CONTROL

More than a decade before the DC Scale was published, Julian Rotter developed and published what for many years was perhaps the most popular trait measure used in personality research. As part of his social learning theory, Rotter (1966) introduced the idea of *generalized expectancies*. He argued that people could be placed along a continuum on the extent to which they typically see what happens to them as under their own control or under the control of external forces. At one end of the dimension we find internals, who generally maintain that whether people get ahead in the world, make friends, clean up government, and control society's problems is largely under their own control. At the other end we find externals, who generally believe that there is little one can do to influence these events. They maintain instead that people in powerful positions and good and bad luck often are the determinants of their fates.

I am frequently asked how desire for control differs from Rotter's locus of control concept. Theoretically, the difference seems apparent. Whereas locus of control is concerned with the extent to which people *perceive* they are in control, desire for control is concerned with the extent to which people *want* control. Thus, a person can have an external locus of control, but a high desire for control. A worker slaving under an authoritarian boss may perceive that he or she has very little control over what happens during working hours. However, this person may very well have a strong desire to one day become the one calling the shots.

On the other hand, one could argue that the person who has a strong desire to be his or her own boss will eventually figure out a way to obtain that control. Similarly, people who have a low desire for control will seek out and be satisfied in situations in which they have little say over what happens to them. In other words, a case can be made that eventually the amount of control people typically prefer will correspond fairly well with the amount of control they perceive they have.

However, a reasonable case can be made for the opposite pattern as well. Perhaps a strong desire for control results from persistent frustration in exercising control. This analysis is consistent with Brehm's (1966) theory of psychological reactance. Brehm maintains that people respond to perceived threats to their freedom with an increased motivation to exercise that freedom. Thus, people who are told that they may not do something respond by doing just the opposite of what they are told. When we apply this analysis, we might expect a negative correlation between desire for control and locus of control measures.

Fortunately, a fairly clear empirical answer to this question has emerged. As shown in Table 2-1, correlations between the DC Scale and general measures of locus of control indicate low to moderate correlations between the concepts. Rotter's original Internal–External Scale seems only weakly related to the DC Scale. Levenson's (1981) scales divide locus of control into three components: the extent to which people believe that what happens to them is the result of their own actions (Internal), the acts of powerful other people (Powerful Others), and simply good or bad luck (Chance). As shown in the table, a high desire for control score is moderately associated with a belief that what happens is the result of personal action and not the actions of powerful others or chance.

Other information about the relationship between desire for control and locus of control comes from research with specific, as contrasted with general, locus of control measures. A number of researchers have

TABLE 2-1. Correlations between DC Scale and Locus of Control Measures

Scale	Sample	N	r	Reference
Rotter I-E Scale	College students	268	−.19	Burger & Cooper (1979)
	Male college students	67	−.11	Dembroski et al. (1984)
Levenson Chance Scale	College students	392	−.29	Zimmerman & Rappaport (1988)
	Adults (mean age 41.94)	176	−.21	Zimmerman & Rappaport (1988)
	College students	98	−.36	Burger (1984)
	College students	63	−.04	Crowe & Burger (1984)
Levenson Internal Scale	College students	392	.47	Zimmerman & Rappaport (1988)
	Adults (mean age 41.94)	176	.32	Zimmerman & Rappaport (1988)
	College students	98	.46	Burger (1984)
Levenson Powerful Others Scale	College students	392	−.33	Zimmerman & Rappaport (1988)
	Adults (mean age 41.94)	176	−.27	Zimmerman & Rappaport (1988)
	College students	98	−.36	Burger (1984)

developed scales to examine perceived control for specific kinds of events, such as locus of control for academic achievement (Crandall, Katkovsky, & Crandall, 1965) and health behavior (Wallston & Wallston, 1981). Although these measures are related to a general perception of being able to influence events, they provide for better prediction of behavior in the specific domain of interest.

Several researchers report correlations between scores on the DC Scale and the Multidimensional Health Locus of Control (MHLC) Scale (Wallston & Wallston, 1981). Like Levenson's general locus of control scales, the MHLC Scale measures the extent to which test takers tend to see control over their health as a function of their own actions (Internal Scale), other people (Powerful Others Scale) or simply chance (Chance Scale). Correlations among these scales and the DC Scale reported from two studies are shown in Table 2-2.

Paulhus (1983) divided locus of control into three spheres of control. He argues that people can feel more or less control over personal achievements (Personal Efficacy), over interactions with others (Interpersonal Control), and over the political and social system (Sociopolitical Control). I correlated scores on each of these scales with the DC Scale scores of a group of undergraduate students. The results of this unpublished study are shown in Table 2-3. As seen in the table, I found moderate correlations between desire for control and subjects' belief that they could exercise control over all three of these areas of their lives.

In summary, evidence from correlations with general as well as specific measures of locus of control suggests that whereas a high desire for control tends to be related to an internal locus of control, the correlation is modest. It is quite possible for someone to have a high desire for control and be an external, and to find someone with a low desire for control who maintains an internal locus of control. Further, a few studies have compared the two constructs and have found that individual differences in desire for control sometimes predict behaviors that locus of control does not. For example, Zimmerman and Rappaport

TABLE 2-2. Correlations between DC Scale and Health Locus of Control Scales

Scale	Sample	N	r	Reference
Internal Scale	Adults	246	−.15	Woodard et al. (1983)
Chance Scale	Adults	246	−.20	Woodard et al. (1983)
Powerful Others Scale	Adults	246	−.21	Woodard et al. (1983)
Internal Scale	Cardiovascular patients	17	.14	Hatton et al. (1989)
Chance Scale	Cardiovascular patients	17	−.01	Hatton et al. (1989)
Powerful Others Scale	Cardiovascular patients	17	−.45	Hatton et al. (1989)

TABLE 2-3. Correlations between DC Scale Scores
and the Paulhus Spheres of Control Scales

Scale	Males	Females	Total
Personal efficacy	.44**	.26	.34**
Interpersonal control	.52**	.42**	.45**
Sociopolitical control	.28*	.31*	.30**

Note: Sample = 37 males and 39 females; * $p < .05$; ** $p < .01$

(1988) found that desire for control predicted whether people became involved in community projects, whereas some measures of locus of control did not. Similarly, Hatton, Gilden, Edwards, Cutler, Kron, and McAnulty (1989) found that desire for control scores identified patients at high risk for sudden cardiac death, whereas measures of health locus of control produced no significant relationship. Finally, at times it may be useful to identify people who have, for example, a high desire for control yet maintain an external locus of control. As described in Chapter 8, this group has been found to be at higher risk for depression. In short, desire for control should be thought of as a personality construct related to but different than locus of control.

TYPE A BEHAVIOR

Another personality construct conceptually similar to desire for control is known as coronary-prone behavior pattern, or, more simply, Type A personality. A large amount of literature on this concept describes the Type A individual as one who is driven to achieve, overcome obstacles, and beat the competition. Type A people are easily aroused to anger, time conscious, and sometimes power hungry. Type B people, on the other end of this personality dimension, are said to experience these behaviors much less often and in much lower intensity.

The notion of a Type A personality pattern was originally hypothesized and developed by medical researchers trying to predict which patients were at high risk for heart attacks (Friedman & Rosenman, 1974). Several early investigations indicated that Type A people were more likely than Type Bs to suffer from cardiovascular problems. Although subsequent research indicates that this is not always the case and that perhaps one or more components that make up the Type A syndrome may be responsible for the link to health problems (Dembroski & Costa, 1987), there is ample evidence that some relationship between Type A personality and health exists.

However, personality psychologists soon discovered that Type A people also differed from Type Bs on a large number of predictable behavioral measures. Reviewing this vast literature is well beyond the scope of this book, but one very relevant aspect of this research deserves mention. Glass (1977), summarizing a program of research on the Type A construct, concluded that the key difference between people classified as Type A and Type B was a difference in "strategy for coping with uncontrollable aversive events." In other words, Glass proposed that the one thread tying all of the characteristic Type A behaviors together might be a strong motivation to exercise control over the environment.

It is important to point out that this interpretation of the Type A construct was developed after the scales to measure this personality dimension were constructed, as contrasted with the DC Scale, which was developed from the start with the purpose of assessing individual differences in desire for control. Nonetheless, if Glass is correct, we would expect that scores from Type A measures to correlate at least moderately with scores on the DC Scale.

What is the empirical relationship between desire for control and Type A personality? As shown in Table 2-4, a fairly clear pattern has emerged in research examining this question. The table shows a consistent moderate correlation between the DC Scale and measures of Type A personality, with higher Type A scores associated with higher desire for control scores. This seems to be the case regardless of how Type A personality is assessed.

Additional evidence for this relationship comes from research reported by Rhodewalt and Marcroft (1988), who compared Type A and Type B diabetic patients on each of the five factors reported in our initial factor analysis of the DC Scale. They found Type As scored significantly

TABLE 2-4. Correlations between DC Scale and Measures of Type A Behavior

Scale	Sample	N	r	Reference
Structured Interview	Male college students	70	.24	Musante et al. (1983)
Jenkins Activity Survey	Male college students	70	.37	Musante et al. (1983)
	College students	200	.46	Smith & O'Keeffe (1985)
	College students	39	.39	Burger (1985)
	Cardiovascular patients	17	.68	Hatton et al. (1989)
	Female college students	69	.26	Lawler et al. (1990)
	College students	98	.37	Burger (unpublished)
	College students	84	.49	Strube (unpublished)
Framingham Type A Scale	College students	200	.22	Smith & O'Keeffe (1985)

higher on the General Desire for Control factor and the Avoidance of Dependence factor than Type Bs.

Although the pattern presented in the table gives a fairly clear and consistent picture, a few exceptions have been reported. Musante, Mac-Dougall, Dembroski, and Van Horn (1983) failed to find a significant correlation between desire for control and an overall Type A score for the female subjects in their sample. However, they do report significant correlations between desire for control and some of the Type A component scores for these women. Lawler, Schmied, Armstead, and Lacy (1990) report a significant correlation between desire for control and Type A personality when using the Jenkins Activity Survey, but not when they measured Type A personality with the Framington Type A Scale with a sample of female undergraduates. Heft et al. (1988) modified the desire for control scale for administration to fifth, seventh, and ninth graders. They report no significant differences between the Type A and Type B children in their sample. Finally, Wright (1988) states that he has not found significant correlations between Type A personality and desire for control, but he does not indicate which instruments he used or the strength of the correlations.

Nonetheless, there appears to be consistent evidence that desire for control and Type A personality are moderately related. I interpret this evidence to mean that a high desire for control is one of the components that make up the typical Type A personality pattern. However, Type A personality and desire for control are not the same concepts. Type A personality is concerned with a pattern of behaviors, and debate continues as to what motives underlie these behaviors and whether or not it is correct or useful to lump several behaviors together under the concept of a *behavior pattern*. Desire for control is concerned with a general motivation to control the events in one's environment. To illustrate the importance of this distinction, we can point to the research described in Chapter 9 on gambling behavior. We have predicted and found some evidence that desire for control is related to certain kinds of gambling behavior. It is reasonable to make this prediction because we argue that one of the motives affecting the perception and behavior of the gambler is a need for control. However, there is no similar reason to predict people with the Type A behavior pattern would be more likely to gamble than Type Bs.

Additional information about the relationship between desire for control and Type A personality comes from researchers who have broken the Type A construct into some of the components that seem to make up this behavior pattern. For example, Lawler et al. (1990) found significant correlations between desire for control and the Job Involvement

(r = .34) and Hard Driving and Competitive (r = .48) subscales of the Jenkins Activity Survey among college age women. However, these researchers found no correlation between desire for control and the Speed and Impatience subscale (r = .05). Hatton *et al.* (1989) also looked at these components of the Jenkins Activity Survey with a sample of largely male cardiovascular patients. They found significant correlations between desire for control and the Job Involvement (r = .52), Hard Driving and Competitive (r = .40), and Speed and Impatience (r = .71) scores. Musante *et al.* (1983) looked at component scores derived from the structured interview procedure. They found significant correlations between desire for control and the Pressured Drive (r = .25) and Anger (r = .31) components for male subjects. For the females in their sample, significant correlations were found between desire for control and the Pressured Drive (r = .30), Impatience (r = .42), and Speed of Activity (r = .23) components.

In summary, desire for control and Type A personality are related to one another in predictable ways. The magnitude of the correlations suggests that people scoring high on one scale will tend to score high on the other. I interpret this correlation to mean that a high desire for control is one of the components or symptoms of the overall Type A behavior pattern. However, the correlations also tend to be low enough to make it useful to examine DC Scale scores and Type A scores separately. As in the discussion about locus of control, we can illustrate the importance of distinguishing between desire for control and Type A personality by looking at a few studies that find different patterns of results for Type A personality and desire for control scores. For example, one study found that whereas desire for control was related to how hard subjects worked on a challenging task, Type A personality was not (Burger, 1985). Similarly, Hatton *et al.* (1989) found desire for control significantly predicted which cardiovascular patients were at risk for sudden cardiac death, whereas their measures of Type A personality did not. These researchers even found an interaction between Type A personality and desire for control for one of the physiological measures they examined. Although the interpretation of this effect remains unclear, desire for control subjects who also were classified as Type Bs were more likely than any other group to produce high levels of epinephrine when experiencing cardiovascular stress. Similarly, Lawler *et al.* (1990) found several meaningful interactions between Type A personality and desire for control when examining physiological reactivity to mildly stressful situations. In short, it is important to retain the distinction between desire for control and Type A personality.

SOCIAL DESIRABILITY

As with any personality scale, it is important to demonstrate that people completing the DC Scale are not merely responding with answers they believe to be the most socially acceptable. Demonstrating discriminant validity from measures of social desirability is especially important for the DC Scale because several people (usually those with a high desire for control) have suggested to me that all people are supposed to want personal control in our society and that no one will admit to not wanting control. Fortunately, the empirical evidence does not support this speculation. I have correlated the DC Scale with measures of social desirability in three different samples. As shown in Table 2-5, the same results emerged each time. That is, there is little, if any, relationship between desire for control and social desirability. Thus, we can have confidence that subjects scoring high on the scale are not merely responding as they believe they are supposed to, but rather probably have a generally higher need to control the events in their lives than those scoring low.

NEED FOR CONTROL/POWER SCALES

Two personality scales that might be related to the DC Scale were suggested by several people who first heard about the desire for control construct. These are the FIRO-B Scale and the Machiavellian Scale. The Fundamental Interpersonal Relations Orientation-Behavior (FIRO-B) Scale was developed by Will Schutz (1977) in his work with encounter groups. Among the scores available from this test are some that measure the extent to which people generally dominate other people, make decisions, and assume responsibility in social situations. Scores can be derived for Expressed Control, the test takers' overt behavior, and Wanted Control, what the test takers would prefer. In contrast to the DC Scale, which was developed to measure a general desire for control, the FIRO-B is concerned with control as it relates to interpersonal relations (Ryan, 1970). Nonetheless, we would expect that high desire for

TABLE 2-5. Correlations between DC Scale and Measures of Social Desirability

Scale	Sample	N	r	Reference
Marlowe–Crowne Social Desirability	College students	360	.11	Burger & Cooper (1979)
Marlowe–Crowne Social Desirability	College students	106	.10	Burger (unpublished)
Eysenck Personality Inventory, Lie Scale	College students	176	.07	Burger (unpublished)

control people would exercise a great deal of control and prefer to exercise a great deal of control over their social interactions as well as other parts of their lives.

The Machiavellian Scale was developed by Christie and Geis (1970). These researchers were interested in measuring the extent to which a person characteristically manipulates other people to achieve his or her own goals. People scoring high on measures of Machiavellianism are said to have little emotional involvement or moral and ideological concerns, but rather are primarily interested in getting others to do what they want. Although the researchers approached their study of Machiavellianism from a very different perspective than the one from which the desire for control construct was developed, we could speculate that people scoring high on one scale might also score high on the other.

I administered the two control subscales from the FIRO-B Scale, the Machiavellian IV Scale, and the DC Scale to an undergraduate sample. The results of this unpublished study are shown in Table 2-6. The FIRO-B scales were related to desire for control in predictable ways. Subjects with a high desire for control express and want control over their social interactions. Contrary to expectation, scores on the DC Scale were not related to Machiavellianism. The latter finding may have to do with the rather narrow aspect of control tapped by the Machiavellian scale. That is, the scale deals primarily with a need to manipulate people and satisfy a craving for power. Although such motives may represent one way a high desire for control is expressed, this is probably not very common.

OTHER CONTROL-RELATED MEASURES

Several researchers have developed other personality scales designed to measure control-related concepts. As shown in Table 2-7, several of these researchers have reported correlations between these scales and the DC Scale. In general, the pattern of correlations shown in the table is approximately what I would have predicted. That is, although each of the scales is measuring something conceptually similar to desire for con-

TABLE 2-6. Correlations between
DC Scale and Scales Measuring Similar Constructs

Scale	Males	Females	Total Sample
FIRO-B Control Expressed	.40*	.36*	.39**
FIRO-B Control Wanted	−.35*	−.48**	−.41**
MACH-IV Scale (Machiavellianism)	.10	−.12	−.03

Note: Sample = 51 male undergraduates and 55 female undergraduates; * $p < .01$; ** $p < .001$

TABLE 2-7. Correlations between
DC Scale and Various Control-Relevant Personality Scales

Scale	Construct	r	p	Reference
Critical Parent Scale from ACL	Transactional Analysis ego state, parental values	.06	ns	Williams et al. (1983)
Krantz Health Opinion Survey: Behavior	Preference to be involved in one's health care	.01 .12 .35	ns ns .001	Smith et al. (1984)
Krantz Health Opinion Survey: Information	Preference to have information about one's health care	.25 .22 .29	.001 .01 .001	Smith et al. (1984)
Desire for Control of Health Care	Patient's desire for control over health care	.23 .13 .30	.001 ns .001	Smith et al. (1984)
Personal Interest Questionnaire: Motivation	Motivation to work on tasks typically used in learning helplessness experiments	.34	.05	Barber et al. (1986)
Expressed Self-Control	Amount of self-control expressed	.18	ns	Ganong & Coleman (1987)
Yielded Self-Control	How frequently one accepts what happens	−.04	ns	Ganong & Coleman (1987)

Note: Smith et al. (1984) report data from three different studies

trol, there are also important differences between the concepts. Thus, it is not surprising to find that higher desire for control scores are related to a higher motivation to get involved in and find out information about one's health care. This is exactly the kind of behavior we would expect from high desire for control people, who want to control many of the events affecting their personal health just as they want to control many other events in their lives. However, again because we are interested in measuring a general desire for control across many situations and the Krantz scale reported in Table 2-7 is limited to control over health care situations, it is appropriate that the scales correlate only modestly.

OTHER PERSONALITY CONSTRUCTS

To obtain a quick look at how desire for control relates to individual differences in other needs, I looked at the correlations between the DC Scale and scores from the Edwards Personal Preference Schedule (EPPS). The EPPS was developed by Edwards (1959) to assess 15 of the psychogenic needs outlined by Henry Murray (1938). Both personality tests were administered to a group of undergraduates in this unpublished study. As seen in Table 2-8, only a few of the EPPS scores were related to desire for control. However, the few significant correlations that did

TABLE 2-8. Correlations between DC Scale
and Edwards Personal Preference Schedule Need Percentile Scores

Need	Males	Females	Total Sample
Achievement	−.08	.08	.04
Deference	−.39*	−.12	−.26*
Order	−.03	.12	.03
Exhibition	−.08	−.11	−.09
Autonomy	.12	−.13	.00
Affiliation	−.14	−.18	−.15
Intraception	.17	.13	.17
Succorance	−.12	−.24	−.16
Dominance	.44**	.22	.33**
Abasement	−.14	.12	−.02
Nurturance	−.09	−.20	−.12
Change	.06	−.11	−.04
Endurance	−.21	.34*	.07
Heterosexuality	.01	−.10	−.05
Aggression	.22	−.13	.00

Note: Sample = 35 male undergraduates, 35 female undergraduates; * $p < .05$; ** $p < .01$

emerge make some sense. High desire for control males have a higher need for dominance (control over interpersonal relationships) than males with a low desire for control. These high desire for control males have a complementary low need to show deference to higher status people and people in authority. Interestingly, the only significant correlation for the female subjects was a positive correlation with need for endurance, perhaps reflecting a difference in the strategies used by high desire for control men and women to get what they want.

A few people have also suggested to me that desire for control may be nothing more than a variation of Eysenck's well-researched extraversion–introversion concept. Conceptually, the constructs are quite different. Hans Eysenck (1982) describes extraverts as people who are in constant need of cortical arousal. Extraverts satisfy this need through a variety of sources. One common means of satisfying this need is to engage in more social activities than the introverts found at the other end of the personality dimension. But would extraverts or introverts have a higher desire for control? It is possible that the highly sociable extraverts are very interested in controlling the behavior of others. On the other hand, I could speculate that introverts, concerned about limiting their amount of cortical arousal, would be more interested than extraverts in controlling their environments.

To answer this question, I administered the DC Scale and the Eysenck Personality Inventory (EPI) (Eysenck & Eysenck, 1968) to a group of undergraduates in an unpublished study. The EPI provides scores for extraversion–introversion and for the personality dimension neuroticism. According to Eysenck, people who score high on neuroticism are "emotionally overresponsive and . . . have difficulties in returning to a normal state after emotional experiences" (Eysenck & Eysenck, 1968). As shown in Table 2-9, only small and nonsignificant correlations between desire for control and both extraversion and neuroticism were found.

Although desire for control does not seem to be related to extraversion, one researcher did find slight correlations between desire for control and some aspects of sensation seeking, a trait conceptually similar to extraversion. Hayes (1988) administered the DC Scale and the Sensation Seeking Scale, Form V (Zuckerman, 1979) to a large group of undergraduates. He found a small but significant correlation between the two scales ($r = .20$, $p < .01$), with a high desire for control associated with higher sensation seeking. In addition, a high desire for control was associated with the Thrill and Adventure Seeking ($r = .26$, $p < .01$) and the Experience Seeking ($r = .16$, $p < .05$) subscale scores from the Sensation Seeking Scale. Thus, although the correlations are relatively small, there may be some relation between sensation seeking and desire for control.

In summary, a large number of correlations from several studies indicate that the DC scale correlates slightly or moderately with a large number of personality scales. The pattern of these correlations is consistent with the notion that people scoring high on the DC Scale generally have a higher need to control the events in their environments than people scoring low on the scale. In short, this research demonstrates good discriminant and convergent validity for the DC Scale.

DEMOGRAPHIC VARIABLES
RELATED TO DESIRE FOR CONTROL SCORES

A few researchers have reported relationships between desire for control and various demographic variables. Although much more re-

TABLE 2-9. Correlations between DC Scale Scores and Scores on the Eysenck Personality Inventory

Scale	Males	Females	Total
Extraversion	.04	.13	.09
Neuroticism	−.12	−.03	−.08

Note: Sample = 90 males and 86 females; all rs not significant

search needs to be conducted in each of these areas, some data exist relating desire for control to gender, age, and education.

GENDER DIFFERENCES

Do men or women have a higher desire for control? A clear answer to this question is suggested from popular commentaries about gender differences. Men in our society are supposed to be raised with a much stronger need to exercise control. They are said to have a higher need to achieve, to dominate, to act aggressively, to make the decisions, and to be independent. In contrast, women are supposed to be more dependent and less achievement oriented. Many women's groups have encouraged assertiveness training to help women overcome the effects of this socialization. Much empirical research points in the same direction. For example, look at some of the adjectives used for the Masculinity and Femininity scales on the Bem Sex Role Inventory (Bem, 1974). Test takers are considered masculine if they describe themselves with the following terms: aggressive, assertive, dominant, has leadership abilities, independent, makes decisions easily, self-reliant, and self-sufficient. On the other hand, a high score on femininity is obtained if the test taker endorses self-descriptions such as flatterable, gullible, shy, soft spoken, and yielding. All these observations suggest that men should average significantly higher scores on the DC Scale than women.

However, the empirical findings are not so dramatic. We found a slight tendency for males to have a higher desire for control than females in our original sample of college undergraduates (Burger & Cooper, 1979). The men averaged about four and a half points higher on the 140-point scale than the women. Because of the large sample size, this difference was statistically significant. When we examined gender differences in our samples in several subsequent investigations with college students we typically found even smaller, often nonsignificant, differences between male and female college students. Means reported by other investigators also indicate a small, but sometimes detectable, gender difference among college students.

Do these results mean that American men have a slightly higher desire for control than women? Perhaps. But recall that the data discussed thus far concern college students who, as nearly all psychologists are aware, often are not representative of the population as a whole. Although no study has tested this hypothesis directly, as I look at the data from a number of investigations examining a number of different populations, I believe I see a pattern emerging. That pattern suggests that gender differences in desire for control may be a function of age.

That is, younger adults, most notably college students, who have been raised in an environment emphasizing the need for women to become more assertive and self-reliant, show relatively small desire for control differences between men and women. However, older adults, socialized under different standards for male and female behavior, are more likely to show the traditional gender–role pattern of men having a higher desire for control than women.

Although there is not an abundance of data to support this latter observation, what gender difference data there are from older samples is fairly consistent. Smith, Woodward, Wallston, Wallston, Rye, and Zylstra (1988) examined desire for control scores in a sample of adults with an average age of 46.9 years. They report a significant difference between males and females, with males scoring higher in desire for control. They also broke their sample into three age groups (20 to 39, 40 to 59, 60 and older) and found no interaction with age, indicating that the gender difference did not change across the adult age groups. Smith et al. (1984) report correlations of −.31 ($p < .001$) and −.30 ($p < .001$) between gender and DC scores when examining adult samples with mean ages of 49.67 and 44.20 years, respectively. Again, the correlations indicate that the males in the samples had higher DC scores than the females. Schönbach's (1990) data with various German subjects uncovered similar gender differences among adult samples. He found male subjects scored significantly higher than females on the DC Scale when administering the test to secondary school teachers ($p < .05$) and to a random sample of adults in the community ($p < .10$). Thus, when researchers look at gender differences with adult samples, they consistently find evidence that men score higher on the DC Scale than women.

But what about younger samples, boys and girls not yet in college? Schönbach (1990) also reports data from a group of 15- to 16-year-old students in his German sample. Although the males in the sample have a slightly higher mean than the females, the difference falls short of significance. Heft et al. (1988) administered a modified version of the DC Scale to children in the fifth, seventh, and ninth grades. They report virtually identical scores for the boys and girls.

Taken together, the data from all these samples support the speculation that gender differences in desire for control are related to age. Males and females who went through gender role socialization a generation or so ago (that is, postcollege adults today) tend to reflect the traditional gender role notion of males wanting to exercise more control over their environments than females. However, college students do not always show this pattern, and the little data we have on very young samples (recent high school and junior high school students) show virtually no gender differences at all. What these findings suggest is that society may be slowly letting go of the traditional gender roles that teach men to be dominant and controlling and women dependent and non-assertive. If this hypothesis is correct and the process continues, we may expect little or no gender differences in the extent to which males and females want control over the events in their lives in the future.

Of course, this conclusion is based on cross-sectional, rather than longitudinal, data. To my knowledge, only one study has investigated changes in desire for control through a longitudinal design. As mentioned earlier, a colleague and I recently compared DC Scale scores for male and female subjects over a 10-year period (Burger & Solano, 1991). People who completed the DC Scale as undergraduates in 1980 also completed the scale in 1990. The males in the sample scored significantly higher than the females in 1980, with almost a standard deviation between the means for the two groups. The males' scores did not change appreciably over the 10-year period. However, the females' scores increased dramatically during the decade of the 1980s. In fact, the women's scores increased to the point where they were no longer significantly different from the men's scores.

At this point interpreting these data remains very speculative. Clearly the typical woman in this sample significantly increased her desire for control score between 1980 and 1990. Why might this be the case? It could be something about the decade that made the women come to see the importance of exercising control over their lives. This interpretation would be consistent with the goals of the women's movement during these years. It also is possible that something about the typical experiences of college-educated American females between ages 20 and 30 leads to an increase in desire for control. Leaving school, getting out in the business world, and perhaps starting a family might all contribute to this effect. Although a complete understanding of this finding remains elusive for now, these data again underscore the notion that gender differences in desire for control need to be examined in terms of the age of the subjects.

AGE

Although gender may play a role in changes in desire for control over time, is there a general relation we can point to between desire for control and age? For example, do people early in their careers have a stronger need to demonstrate mastery over the challenges of life than the elderly who have already passed this stage of life? Or do the increases in health problems and decline in some physical abilities associated with aging lead to an increased need to exercise some control? Relevant data for these questions come from several investigations that examined age differences in desire for control through cross-sectional procedures. Unfortunately, no clear answers emerge from these studies.

Smith et al. (1984) examined correlations between age and desire for control with three separate groups of adults. They found a slightly positive correlation between DC score and age for one sample of young adult women ($r = .18$) and another sample of male and female adults ($r = .11$). However, these researchers also report a slightly negative correlation with age in a third sample of adults ($r = -.17$). Woodward and Wallston (1987) administered a modified version of the DC Scale to adults in three age groups: 20 to 39 years, 40 to 59 years, and 60 and over. They found a large drop in desire for control scores for the subjects aged 60 and over as compared with the two younger groups. This difference remained even when scores from a general self-efficacy measure were used as a covariate in the analysis.

However, Smith et al. (1988) compared DC scores for subjects in the same three age groups and found no significant difference between the older subjects and the two younger groups. Woodward and Wallston (1987) speculate that the difference between their findings and the Smith et al. (1988) data may have to do with differences in socioeconomic status of the two samples. They suggest that Smith et al. (1988) may have failed to find a decrease in desire for control in their older subjects because they sampled men and women with relatively high socioeconomic status. These elderly with high socioeconomic status may see themselves as having the financial ability and opportunities to exercise effective control that elderly with lower socioeconomic status do not. Finally, Braukmann (1981) found little evidence for differences in mean desire for control scores across age groups in his sample of German citizens.

In short, to date there is little indication that people maintain a higher level of desire for control at one age than they do at any other. However, what may be most striking about these data is that, contrary to what is suggested by research in other areas, there is no clear indication of a dropoff in general desire for control among the elderly. This conclusion is especially noteworthy in that Smith et al. (1984) found evidence that the desire to exercise control specifically over one's health care is significantly lower among the elderly than among the younger people in their samples. This finding indicates that the situation-specific desire for control construct, while more predictive of health-related behaviors than a general measure of desire for control, may also be more susceptible to changes. This observation makes sense if we think of people's general desire for control level as made up of their need for control over all aspects of their lives. For a number of reasons, such as a series of health setbacks, an elderly person may decide to relinquish control of his or her health care to a more qualified professional. However, that person might still want to control many of the other aspects of his or her life.

EDUCATION

The relationship between desire for control and education level has been examined in four studies by Roberta Smith and her colleagues. First, Smith *et al.* (1984) reported a positive correlation between DC Scale scores and education in each of three investigations. These correlations ranged from .22 to .29, indicating that the higher one's education, the higher the desire for control. Consistent with these findings, Smith *et al.* (1988) found a positive correlation of .24 in a fourth sample of adults. Thus, although few in number, the studies provide consistent evidence that a modest but significant relationship exists between desire for control and education level.

We can speculate about many reasons why high desire for control people would tend to have more formal education than people with a low desire for control. My preferred interpretation is that high desire for control people see achievement tasks, including education, as a means of demonstrating competence and mastery, and perhaps even as a challenge to their sense of personal control. Consequently, I would expect high desire for control students to do better in school and to reach higher levels of educational achievement than students with a low desire for control. As described in Chapter 5, several studies find that high desire for control people have a higher need for achievement and tend to do better on achievement tasks. One of these studies found that high desire for control students performed better in college classes than students with a low desire for control.

However, as with any correlational analysis, alternate causal relationships may be operating. It is possible that higher educational achievement contributes to a higher desire for control. Perhaps the reinforcement that comes with academic success or the years of exposure to a system emphasizing tests, grades, academic challenges, and performance help to develop a need to meet those challenges and conquer them. Indeed, many graduate students have commented on how they become caught up and immersed in academic performance. Finally, the desire for control–education link may be the result of a third variable, such as socio-economic status or self-esteem, that relates to both desire for control and educational achievement.

SUMMARY

The research reviewed in this chapter not only demonstrates that the Desirability of Control Scale is a reliable and valid instrument for measuring individual differences in need for control, it also tells us much about the nature of the desire for control construct. Internal consistency and test–retest data tell us rather conclusively that the DC Scale is a fairly reliable instrument. The pattern of correlations from numerous studies and samples illustrates how desire for control fits in with the network of other personality dimensions and traits investigated by personality researchers. Knowing a person's level of desire for control allows us to make some guess about how he or she would score on other personality measures. For example, a person with a higher desire for control is more likely than not to have a Type A personality pattern and prefer to have control over his or her personal health decisions.

Perhaps more important, the pattern of correlations demonstrates that the desire for control construct is distinctive from many seemingly related personality constructs. For example, desire for control is not the same as locus of control, Machiavellianism, or extraversion. Scores on the DC Scale do not correlate with measures of social desirability. In other words, although it may be related to other personality traits, a general desire for control is an important and distinct personality construct.

Finally, some interesting hypotheses can be generated from the data relating desire for control to gender, age, and education. Differences between men and women on desire for control may reflect the type of gender–role socialization that the generation in the sample experienced. However, recent longitudinal data hint that life experiences also can significantly alter desire for control levels among adults, particularly among women. We also must resort to speculation to account for the finding that a high desire for control is related to higher levels of education. In all probability this correlation is the result of many causal links.

In conclusion, the Desirability of Control Scale provides researchers with a psychometrically sound method to assess individual differences in the extent to which people generally prefer to control the events in their lives. The remainder of this book is devoted to examining how those individual differences are related to a wide range of behaviors.

CHAPTER 3

SOCIAL INTERACTIONS

Few aspects of our lives are as pervasive or as important to us as our interpersonal relationships. We consistently put our relationships with friends, family members, and romantic partners at or near the top of the list of what is most important in our lives and what makes us happy (Argyle, 1987). Since as far back as any of us can remember, interactions with others have played such a central role in our daily lives that an absence of social contact for an extended period of time is considered unusual, if not abnormal. Shyness and loneliness are problems that may require professional intervention. Psychologists often consider a reduction in social interaction a sign of depression or some other psychological disorder. People who prefer excessive amounts of time to themselves are objects of curiosity.

Because our relationships play such an important role in our lives, it is reasonable to ask if individual differences in desire for control might be related to our social interactions. Control quite probably becomes an issue in many of our daily conversations. That is, interactions often have a purpose beyond having a pleasant social encounter. We may want information or a favor from this person. Further, if a decision is to be made, there is the issue of who decides or how much each person will influence the decision. Other control-relevant agenda items can surface in social interactions, such as when we are concerned about being manipulated by the person we are dealing with, or if we want to change this person's attitude or behavior. And in most cases there is the underlying concern for controlling what this other person thinks of us. In short, there are many reasons why a person with a high desire for control might approach social interactions and relationships differently than someone with a low desire for control.

This chapter looks at how individual differences in desire for control affect interpersonal interactions in three areas. First, desire for control may be related to interaction style. That is, people with different levels of desire for control may employ different interaction behaviors in their efforts to increase or decrease a sense of control over the interaction. Next, I look at how people react to conversations with partners with a high desire for control and with low desire for control partners. Are these conversations enjoyable and how well do high desire for control people and low desire for control people gauge what others think of them? Finally, how does desire for control affect our friendships and romantic relationships? Some research indicates that desire for control plays a role in who we choose to interact with, how much we value social contact, and even our sexual behavior.

INTERPERSONAL STYLE

If desire for control plays a role in how we interact with others, what sorts of differences might we expect between high desire for control people and low desire for control people? At least two seemingly inconsistent possibilities can be suggested. Perhaps the more obvious of the two hypotheses is that high desire for control people are more likely than low desire for control people to be dominant in their relationships and dominate their social interactions. Each of us has seen people who take control of a conversation. These people decide what the topic of conversation will be and probably do most of the talking. They may speak louder than anyone else and perhaps even position themselves so as to be literally in the center of the group. It would be an easy leap to guess that such people have a high need to control the conversation. Thus, the first hypothesis about desire for control and interaction style is that high desire for control people are more likely than people with a low desire for control to engage in control-enhancing behaviors when interacting with others.

There are many ways people with a high desire for control might exert control over a conversation. One is to control the conversation topic. Controlling what the conversation is about allows us to avoid topics we find boring, embarrassing, uncomfortable, or that we know little about. People also sometimes want to bring up topics that allow them to show off their knowledge, express a strongly held view, or gain wanted information. Thus, we would expect that high desire for control people would be more likely than low desire for control people to introduce new topics or change the topic of conversation when they have something else they want to talk about.

Another way to control the flow of the conversation is by asking questions. We can direct what our conversation partners say by asking them specifically what we want to know, rather than letting them tell the story the way they might prefer. More directly, people with a high desire for control might simply interrupt their conversation partners when they do not like what the partner is saying or when they want to express their own views on the issue. Control can also be exercised by deciding when and for how long a conversation takes place. Initiating and ending conversations provides more control over how they proceed than waiting for someone else to take these actions. Thus, there are a number of tactics a high desire for control person might use in an effort to control directly what happens during a conversation.

However, the image of high desire for control people actively manipulating the behavior of the people they talk with may be only part of the picture. Social interactions necessarily involve the exchange of information, and at times controlling that information may be important. Would it be better to express how you feel about a controversial issue in a group discussion or wait until you find out how the other people feel first? Should you reveal personal information about yourself or wait until you are sure that your partner can be trusted with this information?

The second hypothesis about the high desire for control interaction style is that these people may be more likely than people with a low desire for control to approach social interactions with a reserved style. That is, they may prefer to collect information about other people first and then use that information to decide about what and how much to reveal about their own views and about themselves. Like experienced poker players who do not want to reveal their hands, high desire for control people may enjoy the advantage that comes from knowing more about someone else than they know about you.

If this second hypothesis is correct, then we would expect that high desire for control people would be less likely than people with a low desire for control to reveal intimate information about themselves. They might also be slow to enter a conversation or group discussion until they have had a chance to learn something about the people they are talking with and perhaps get an idea of how these other people might react. They might even limit how much they talk and monitor closely how others react to what they say.

While both of these descriptions of the interaction style of high desire for control people make sense, they also appear to be contradictory. On the one hand, we picture someone who actively tries to control the flow of the conversation by asking questions, changing topics, and interrupting his or her partner. On the other hand, I have described someone who enters conversations cautiously and is careful about putting too much into the interaction. Can both of these descriptions be correct? Do people with a high need for control jump in and dominate a conversation or do they lay back and allow others to do most of the work? As we will see in the next section, there is evidence that they do both.

THE ACTIVE HIGH DESIRE FOR CONTROL STYLE

If high desire for control people are highly motivated to control their conversations, what might they do to establish and maintain this control? The first evidence for some of the ways high desire for control people seek to control their social interactions comes from an experiment by Dembroski, MacDougall, and Musante (1984). These researchers were interested in the relationship between desire for control and some of the behaviors used to classify people as Type A individuals. They interviewed undergraduate males with a standard interview format used to assess Type A Behavior Pattern (Rosenman, 1978). Judges listened to tape recordings of the interviews and rated the subjects on the extent to which they engaged in five paralinguistic stylistics. These five characteristics were: loud and explosive speech, rapid and accelerated speech, quick responses to the interviewer's comments and questions, potential for hostility, and verbal competitiveness (for example, interrupting the interviewer or speaking at the same time as the interviewer).

The researchers divided subjects into halves, based on their scores from the DC Scale taken a few weeks earlier. As shown in Table 3-1, the two groups differed on four of the five measures. In all cases, the high desire for control subjects exhibited the behavior that was most likely to gain them some control over the interview. They were more likely than

TABLE 3-1. Mean Ratings on Five Speech
Features during an Interview for High Desire
for Control Subjects and Low Desire for Control Subjects

	High DC	Low DC	p
Loud and explosive speech	3.5	2.9	.05
Rapid and accelerated speech	3.7	2.8	.01
Response latency	3.5	2.8	.01
Potential hostility	2.8	2.3	ns
Verbal competitiveness	2.6	1.8	.01

Note: All ratings on a 1 to 5 scale; from Dembroski et al. (1984); reprinted
by permission

low desire for control subjects to be loud and explosive when answering, to speak more rapidly, to respond more quickly to the interviewer, and to interrupt and speak at the same time as the interviewer.

The use of this control-enhancing speech style is particularly interesting in that the interview situation implicitly identifies the interviewer as the one who is in control of much of the interaction. The interviewer is supposed to be the one who asks the questions, probes, and changes topics, while the interviewee's job is to follow the interviewer's lead and provide the information he or she seeks. Yet it may have been the lack of control inherent in this role that led the high desire for control subjects to these control-enhancing behaviors. Talking quickly and interrupting the interviewer may have helped these subjects maintain a sense of control over the situation that was designed to minimize their control.

I examined similar speech patterns in interactions in which neither person was placed in a more powerful role (Burger, 1990). Subjects with a high desire for control and subjects with a low desire for control were selected from the upper and lower 40% of a larger distribution of male undergraduate students who had completed the DC Scale. We then paired subjects into three types of dyads: High DC–High DC, High DC–Low DC, Low DC–Low DC. None of the subjects knew his partner before the experiment. We tape recorded a 10-minute get-acquainted conversation for each dyad. Subjects were told only to carry on the kind of conversation they might if they had just met this person outside of the lab. Judges coded the conversations for the frequency of four behaviors: interrupting one's partner, asking a question, introducing a new topic, and talking at the same time. We reasoned that each of these behaviors might be used to control the conversation.

Several interesting patterns emerged in the data analyses. As shown in Table 3-2, more interruptions occurred when two high desire for control people or two people with a low desire for control interacted than when one high desire for control person and one low desire for control person conversed. A similar pattern was found for the number of simultaneous talking incidents. Both the High DC–High DC dyads ($M = 7.50$)

TABLE 3-2. Frequency of Behaviors as a Function of Dyad Type

	High sub/ High part	High sub/ Low part	Low sub/ High part	Low sub/ Low part
Interrupted partner	5.67	3.58	2.25	8.25
Introduced new topic	2.50	2.50	3.83	4.17

Note: From Burger (1990), Experiment 3; reprinted by permission

and the Low DC–Low DC dyads (M = 9.33) had more of these incidents than the High DC–Low DC pairs (M = 4.38).

That the two high desire for control people felt the need to interrupt one another flows from our predictions. Interrupting the other person and talking at the same time are fairly clear attempts to wrestle away control over who talks and what is being said. However, why the two low desire for control people interrupted one another is more difficult to explain. Perhaps their conversations simply were more awkward, and the interruptions and simultaneous talking represented the failure of either person to establish clear control of the conversation. Another possibility is that these low desire for control people simply lacked the social skills to keep the conversation going smoothly, and instead relied on interruptions when they wanted to make their points.

One other unexpected finding emerged in this study. Subjects with a low desire for control were more likely than high desire for control subjects to introduce new topics. One highly speculative explanation for this finding is that low desire for control people are simply less skilled at controlling a conversation than are people with a high desire for control. Consequently, they may resort to an abrupt and perhaps awkward method of introducing a new topic as a means of talking about what they want to discuss. It is possible that high desire for control people are better able to bring a conversation into line with what they want to say more subtly and smoothly without sudden changes in topic. Although some anomalies remain in these data that require further exploration, the two experiments provide evidence that high desire for control people sometimes engage in control-enhancing behaviors in an effort to actively control their social interactions.

Other evidence in support of this position comes from a study that examined, among other things, how conversations ended. One of the most important decisions people make during their social interactions is when and how to end the interaction. Most of us do not want to end a conversation until we have had the opportunity to finish saying what we want to say or we have obtained the information that led us to initiate the conversation in the first place. We may want a conversation to end because we are bored or uncomfortable with the way it is going. Couples sometimes get into an absurd exchange of words when both people want to have the last word. Clearly, deciding when the conversation has ended can be a powerful tool in controlling social interactions.

I reasoned from such observations that high desire for control people would be more likely than people with a low desire for control to end conversations. To examine this possibility, I recruited undergraduates to keep daily records of their conversations for seven consecutive days

(Burger, 1990). Subjects were asked to describe at the end of each day the longest conversation they had been part of that day. Among the questions subjects answered for each conversation was who had ended the conversation (you, your partner, or both). Subjects did not know that the experiment was related to the DC Scale they had completed earlier. As expected, the high desire for control subjects ($M = 4.12$) ended significantly more of their conversations than subjects with a low desire for control ($M = 3.13$). Thus, ending the conversation appears to be yet another way high desire for control people actively work to control their social interactions.

Other evidence in support of the active control-enhancing hypothesis comes from an unpublished study in which I examined two friends working together. Undergraduate subjects were instructed to bring a close same-gender friend with them to the experiment. Experimenters explained that the subjects would be given descriptions of hypothetical situations that could happen to college students. Their task was to discuss each problem for five minutes and then write on a problem sheet the advice they would give the person in the situation. Two hypothetical situations were used. For each case, the experimenter set the problem sheet containing the description of the situation and the space for the advice midway between the two subjects. The subjects' chairs had been arranged so that the sheet was within an arm's reach of each person, but also so that it was not possible for both subjects to read the problem from where they were sitting.

The placement of the problem sheet was arranged so that we could observe which subject took control of the situation by grabbing the problem sheet. We later had each subject complete the DC Scale, presumably as part of an unrelated study. After eliminating the few instances in which partners scored identically on the DC Scale, or in which two observers could not agree on who physically took control of the problem sheet, we compared the number of times the person with the higher DC

TABLE 3-3. Number of Higher Desire for Control and Lower Desire for Control Partners Who Took the Problem Sheets and Wrote the Dyad's Answers

Behavior	Higher DC partner	Lower DC partner	p value
Took sheet—problem 1	17	9	$p < .08$
Took sheet—problem 2	19	9	$p < .04$
Took sheet—total	36	18	—
Wrote answer—problem 1	13	8	$p < .19$
Wrote answer—problem 2	14	5	$p < .03$
Wrote answer—total	27	13	—

score took the sheet with the number of times the person with the lower DC score grabbed the sheet. These data are presented in Table 3-3. As shown in the table, the partner with the higher DC Scale score physically took control of the sheet twice as often as did the partner with the lower DC score.

We also looked at which partner took control of writing the pairs' advice at the end of the discussion. We reasoned that this behavior also was a way to control the problem-solving encounter. By putting the advice in his or her own words, a high desire for control subject would be better able to control the product of the pair's efforts. We eliminated cases in which both partners had the same DC score or when both partners wrote part of the answer. Consistent with our analysis, as shown in Table 3-3, we found the partner with the higher DC score wrote the answer to the problem more than twice as often as the partner with the lower score.

Taken together, the research reviewed thus far supports the view that people with a high desire for control will actively work to control social interactions, using a variety of methods and strategies. However, as seen in the next section, this research does not mean that these people on occasion are not also more reserved than people with a low desire for control about entering a social encounter and revealing information about themselves.

THE RESERVED HIGH DESIRE FOR CONTROL STYLE

A large amount of research on self-disclosure indicates that people get to know one another through a gradual and reciprocal process of disclosing intimate information about themselves (Derlega & Berg, 1987). This work finds that two strangers typically begin the get-acquainted process by speaking on relatively nonintimate topics, such as what classes they are taking or their plans for the summer. However, as the conversation and the relationship develop, people reveal increasingly personal information about themselves to this other person. The process of self-disclosure continues as long as the two people like one another and as long as each person reveals similarly intimate information about himself or herself. If all goes well, the two people will come to know a great deal of personal information about each other, and an intimate friendship or romantic relationship will develop.

But self-disclosure is not without its dangers. Revealing intimate information to another person can be risky. People we confide in may laugh at our fears, decide they do not like us, or betray our trust by telling our secrets to others. Researchers speculate that one reason for the reciprocal pattern of self-disclosure is that sharing intimate information is a sign of trust—because you have risked revealing this part of yourself with me, I will risk revealing a similarly intimate piece of information about myself.

Thus, while self-disclosing can result in a pleasant social experience, it also can be threatening. From a desire for control perspective, we might say that the risk of revealing information about oneself is tantamount to losing some control over the information and how the relationship will develop. People probably have a much greater sense of control when they hold on to their secrets and reveal potentially damaging information about themselves very selectively. We might predict from this analysis that people with a high desire for control are more careful than low desire for control people about how they reveal intimate information about themselves. A person with a high desire for control may be less likely to self-disclose intimate information until after the other person has self-disclosed.

I examined the relationship between desire for control and self-disclosure in an experiment with college undergraduates (Burger, 1990). We selected subjects from a large pool of undergraduates who had taken the DC Scale earlier. Those students scoring in the top and bottom quarter of the distribution were paired with someone their same gender from the middle half of the distribution. We arranged these dyads so that subjects interacted with someone with a DC Scale score at least 10 points different from their own (an average of 14.8 points apart).

In a modification of a procedure introduced by Davis (1976), subjects were told they would engage in a short, structured get-acquainted conversation. Each subject was given a list of 65 topics, taken from Altman and Taylor (1973), which ranged widely in terms of their intimacy level. Subjects were instructed to take turns selecting and then speaking on one of the topics from the list. They spoke for 60 seconds on each topic until both had spoken 12 times.

When the conversation was over subjects were separated and asked to rate on five-point scales the extent to which they had disclosed personal information on each of their 12 turns. We added the 12 intimacy ratings together to obtain an overall self-disclosure score. As expected, we found that low desire for control subjects reported more self-disclosure than subjects with a high desire for control. The high desire for control subjects appeared to exercise control over what would happen in the interaction by not revealing as much personal information about themselves as did the subjects with a low desire for control. Thus, in this situation high desire for control subjects seemed to adopt the reserved interaction style.

More evidence for a reserved interaction style would be found if high desire for control subjects tended to allow their partners to initiate the conversation. In fact, this is what was found in the unpublished laboratory study described earlier in which two friends discussed what advice to give for a hypothetical problem. Although the partner with the higher desire for control score tended to grab the problem sheet and to write the answer to the problem, this behavior did not necessarily mean that that person offered his or her opinion on the matter first. We examined videotapes of these interactions to determine which member of the pair spoke first for each problem. When one partner had a higher DC Scale score than the other and when both coders agreed on which person had begun to discuss the problem (instead of, for example, an irrelevant nervous comment), we found that the member of the pair with the lower desire for control score was more likely to speak first on both the first and second problem. As shown in Table 3-4, the partner with the higher desire for control score spoke first in only 35% of the cases. Thus, the partner with the higher desire for control score seemed to have waited to express his or her opinion on the matter until first hearing what the other person had to say. By allowing their partners to tip their hand, the high desire for control subjects presumably had more information upon which to base their own presentation. They had the advantage of knowing how their partner felt and perhaps how strongly the partner held that position. This information then helped the subjects with a high desire for control decide how they wanted to proceed. This finding is particularly interesting when we recall that this interaction took place between two friends who presumably are less concerned about saying the wrong thing to one another than they might be if interacting with a stranger.

The results from this last experiment are supported by some data I collected in the study in which we asked undergraduates to keep records of their longest conversation each day for seven consecutive days (Burger, 1990). Recall that the high desire for control subjects in that study were more likely than subjects with a low desire for control to report ending the conversation. However, the high desire for control sub-

TABLE 3-4. Number of Subjects Speaking First on Hypothetical Problems

	Higher desire for control partner	Lower desire for control partner	p value
Spoke first—problem 1	9	17	$p < .08$
Spoke first—problem 2	10	18	$p < .09$
Spoke first—total	19	35	—

jects also reported that they had initiated fewer of these seven conversations (M = 2.71) than did the low desire for control subjects (M = 3.38). Thus, people with a high need for control seem reluctant to begin a long conversation and instead rely on someone else to get things going. However, once the conversation begins, they rely on various techniques to exercise control, such as deciding at what point the conversation will end.

But perhaps the most compelling evidence for the reserved interaction style of high desire for control people comes from an unpublished study in which we listened in on conversations in public settings. The subjects in this study were same-gender pairs of adults who were sitting together carrying on a conversation somewhere on or near Santa Clara University (for example, restaurants, lounge areas). Although we did not ask, most if not all of these people probably were university students. Two trained experimenters sat near enough to overhear the conversation, but did not allow subjects to realize they were listening.

Experimenters listened to five minutes of conversation. If the conversation was interrupted by a third person for a few minutes, the experimenters stopped timing and listening until the two subjects were alone again. If subjects left before five minutes elapsed, they were dropped from the experiment. At the end of the conversation, experimenters estimated the percentage of time each person had spoken. They then approached subjects and explained that they were conducting an experiment about who people choose to sit and talk with. The experimenters asked subjects if they had known one another before the conversation (all had). Each subject was then asked to complete the DC Scale (none refused). The experimenters did not tell subjects their conversation had been overheard.

The two experimenters' estimates of the percentage of time spent talking were highly correlated, r = .85. Where disagreements occurred, we used an average of the two estimates as the subjects' percentage score. When we compared DC scores with the percentage of the conversation subjects had spent talking, a clear pattern emerged. A subject's DC score was negatively correlated with how much he or she had talked, r = −.18. More important, we found a strong negative correlation between how much a subject spoke and the difference between his or her DC score and the partner's DC score, r = −.34. That is, the more a subject's desire for control level was greater than his or her partner's desire for control, the less he or she spoke. This finding suggests that high desire for control people generally prefer to allow their partner to do most of the talking in this type of conversation. If the partner has a low desire for control, the high desire for control person's reserved style may force the partner to do a great deal of the talking.

Thus, there is a persuasive amount of evidence suggesting that high desire for control people are more cautious about entering a conversation and about revealing information about themselves than are people with a low desire for control. It would be very satisfying to say this relatively clear statement about desire for control and social interaction style is always the case. Unfortunately, data from several additional experiments indicate that the relationship is not this simple. We turn to the inconsistencies in the research findings next and some possible resolutions to the issue.

CONVERSATION INITIATION
BY SUBJECTS WITH A HIGH DESIRE FOR CONTROL

Several studies find that people with a high desire for control allow their partners to initiate conversations and do most of the talking. However, other studies find high desire for control people are *more* likely than people with a low desire for control to join in the conversation or express their opinions first. For example, subjects in the self-disclosure experiment were instructed to decide between themselves which one would speak first and which would follow (Burger, 1990). We found that the person in the pair with the higher desire for control score was the one who spoke first in the vast majority of cases.

A similar inconsistency surfaced in the study in which combinations of high desire for control subjects and low desire for control subjects spoke in a short get-acquainted conversation (Burger, 1990). In 9 of the 12 dyads with one high and one low desire for control person, the person with a high desire for control spoke first ($p < .07$). Similarly, in an unpublished study described in detail in the next section, subjects were placed into groups and instructed to discuss ways to improve the American education system. We found the amount that subjects perceived they spoke during the discussion and how much the other members of the group perceived they spoke were positively correlated with their DC Scale scores. In other words, people with a high desire for control did the most talking in this situation.

Thus, some studies find that high desire for control people wait to express their views and do less of the talking, while other studies find high desire for control people speak up right away and often. How can we resolve this apparent inconsistency? A closer examination of these experiments suggests one answer. We have data about who speaks first and who speaks the most from six studies. All three of the studies that find high desire for control people wait to speak examined people interacting with friends and those with whom they were already acquainted. High desire for control subjects in these investigations were less likely than subjects with a low desire for control to initiate conversations in their daily interactions, to speak up in the overheard conversations, and to speak first when working on the hypothetical problems with their friends. However, all three of the studies that find high desire for control people jump right into the conversation and speak frequently looked at pairs of strangers. We found this pattern when subjects chose topics for 60-second self-disclosure speeches, when interacting in a get-acquainted conversation with a stranger, and when discussing the American education system with a group of people they had just met.

This curious and unexpected pattern indicates that the active controlling strategies we find elsewhere are most likely to be utilized by people with a high desire for control when they are first interacting with strangers. Why might this be so? One possibility is that the need to control a social interaction is most prominent when interacting with someone we do not know. When high desire for control people are forced into conversations with strangers, they are unsure about how these other people will act, what these people will think of them, or if they also will try to dominate and control the conversation. In such a control-threatening situation we should not be surprised to find the high desire for control person dive in and actively attempt to control the course and flow of the interaction.

However, when interacting with friends, these same high desire for control people probably feel less of a need to demonstrate control to the other person. Perhaps people with a high desire for control feel comfortable enough with their ability to influence friends and acquaintances when necessary that they do not feel the need to consistently dominate the conversation.

What conclusions can we draw at this point? Clearly, sometimes high desire for control people adopt a strategy of actively trying to control their interactions with others. They may interrupt their partner, speak loud or rapidly, or decide when to end the conversation. However, there are other times when utilizing a more reserved style best meets these people's need to feel in control. They may wait to hear what the other person has to say first or may be very selective about what they reveal about themselves. Quite probably, several variables, such as how familiar they are with their partner, come into play when high desire for control people decide which of these strategies to adopt.

ENJOYMENT AND ACCURACY

The evidence reviewed thus far suggests that interacting with a high desire for control person may be a very different experience than interacting with a person with a low desire for control. This observation leads to some additional questions. First, how enjoyable are conversations with high desire for control people, for both the person high in desire for control and the one interacting with him or her? Second, to what extent are people with a high desire for control aware of how they are perceived by the people they interact with?

How pleasant is it to interact with people who are not very disclosing about themselves, yet who try to control the conversation with a variety of control-enhancing strategies? Some data suggest that interactions with high desire for control people may not be all that enjoyable. I asked subjects in the get-acquainted conversation study to rate how enjoyable they found the 10-minute conversation (Burger, 1990). As shown in Table 3-5, both high and low desire for control subjects enjoyed the conversation more when they interacted with a low desire for control person than when they talked with a high desire for control person; however this preference was particularly true for the subjects with a low desire for control. If, as some of the data suggest, high desire for control people try to dominate conversations with strangers with a variety of techniques, it is not hard to see why low desire for control people find these interactions less than pleasant.

However high desire for control people may not enjoy conversations very much themselves. I asked the students who kept a week-long record of their conversations to rate how pleasant each conversation had been (Burger, 1990). The low desire for control subjects rated their conversations as significantly more pleasant than the subjects with a high desire for control. This finding suggests that high desire for control people either often find social interactions unpleasant, perhaps because of the inherent threat some of these conversations have for their sense of control, or that they simply do not derive as much pleasure from social interactions as do people with a low desire for control. I return to this last point in the next section.

TABLE 3-5. Enjoyment of Get-Acquainted Conversation
as a Function of Own and Partner's Desire for Control Level

	Higher desire for control partner	Lower desire for control partner
High desire for control subject	6.67	7.00
Low desire for control subject	5.17	7.50

Note: Subjects rated enjoyment of the conversation on a 9-point scale, with a higher score indicating more enjoyment; from Burger (1990); reprinted by permission

Do high desire for control people realize what others think of them? I examined this question in an experiment with undergraduate students. In this unpublished study (briefly mentioned earlier), students were randomly assigned to discussion groups comprised of three or four people. We verified ahead of time that none of the students knew one another. The experimenter explained that the study was concerned with the effectiveness of group discussions. The subjects heard that they were to engage in a 15-minute discussion and that they would answer some questions about the experience afterward. All groups spoke on the topic "What are some of the problems with the American education system today and what suggestions do you have for improvements?" The topic was chosen because each subject should have had something to say about it; thus both high desire for control subjects and subjects with a low desire for control should have had an equal opportunity to express their views. Subjects sat in a small circle, with chairs approximately two meters apart. Subjects wore name tags to facilitate learning each others' names. The experimenter sat across the room and did not participate in the discussion.

When 15 minutes elapsed, the experimenter escorted subjects to separate rooms to administer a questionnaire. Subjects were encouraged to be honest on the questionnaire and were assured that none of the other group members would see their responses. The questionnaire contained four pages. Each of the first three pages was identical. Subjects were instructed to list the name of one of the other members of the group at the top of each page. The questions on that page then referred to that person. Subjects were asked to give their impression of each group member on 12 dimensions, using a seven-point scale ranging from not at all to very much for each item. The 12 dimensions were taken from Lewinsohn, Mischel, Chaplin, and Barton (1980) and were: friendly, popular, assertive, attractive, warm, communicates clearly, socially skillful, interested in other people, understands what others say, humorous, speaks fluently, and open and self-disclosing. These 12 ratings were summed to form an overall evaluation of the person's social skills. The questionnaire also asked subjects to rate on a seven-point scale the extent to which they liked that person, and to estimate what percentage of the discussion time that person spent talking.

The last page of the questionnaire asked subjects to evaluate "How you believe you were perceived by the other members of the group during the discussion." Subjects used the same seven-point scale to estimate how the other group members would rate them on the 12 social skills items and how much the other group members like them. Finally, they estimated the percentage of discussion time they spent talking.

All subjects had taken the DC Scale a few weeks before the discussion. First, we compared subjects' perceptions of how they were evaluated by the other subjects with their DC scores. These correlations are shown in Table 3-6. As shown in the table, and as described earlier, the higher the DC score, the more percentage of time the subject spent talking. Both the subject and the other members of the group reported this relationship. Consistent with the results of other experiments, we also found a slight tendency for the other members of the group to dislike subjects as the subject's DC Scale score increased.

How accurate were the high and low desire for control people in estimating how they were perceived by the others in the group? First we calculated the average impression the other three group members had for each subject on each of the dependent variables. We then correlated those impressions with what each subject estimated for the impression he or she had made on the others. As shown in Table 3-7, a mixed package of results emerged. First, the higher the DC score, the greater the disparity between how much subjects thought they were talking and how much time other members of the group thought they had spent talking. A closer examination of the data indicates that *on average* the estimates of the subjects with a high desire for control were fairly close to the estimates made by the other group members. Thus, high need for control subjects did not show a pattern of overestimating or underestimating how much they talked. Rather, they simply were less aware than low desire for control subjects of how much other people perceived they talked.

On the other hand, there was a slight tendency for high desire for control subjects to be *more* accurate than subjects with a low desire for control in estimating how others would rate their social skills and how

TABLE 3-6. Correlations between
DC Scale Scores and Self and Other Estimates

	r with DC Scale
Estimate of how others will rate you	
Social skills	−.19
Like you	.01
Percentage of time talking	.22*
Actual ratings by others	
Social skills	.07
Like you	−.17
Percentage of time talking	.32**

Note: The higher the score, the higher the social skills rating, the
more liking, and the more percentage of time spent talking;
* $p < .10$; ** $p < .05$

TABLE 3-7. Correlations between DC Scale
Scores and Discrepancy between Estimates of
Others' Ratings and Actual Ratings by Others

	r with DC Scale
Social skills	−.16
Liking	−.14
Percentage of time talking	.32*

Note: p < .05

much the other members of the group liked them. In fact, when we
compared subjects with scores in the high and low DC halves, we found
the high-scoring DC subjects had a significantly smaller discrepancy score
($M = 0.63$) than the low-scoring subjects ($M = 1.16$) when estimating how
much the other members of the group liked them, $F (1,36) = 5.80$, $p < .02$.

What can we make of this pattern? Although it is difficult to draw
many strong conclusions from this one experiment, the findings suggest
that while high desire for control people were aware that they spoke
more than the others in this discussion, they did not realize the extent
to which they tended to dominate the conversation. On the other hand,
there is a hint that high desire for control people are more aware than
low desire for control people of how they are perceived by others. We
can speculate that this accuracy also is part of satisfying a high need for
control. Perceiving and understanding subtle feedback about how others
react to us may provide valuable information to someone who is highly
motivated to control that impression or who wants to influence the
behavior of others.

FRIENDSHIPS AND ROMANTIC RELATIONS

Social psychologists have long been interested in how we select
those few people we call friends and lovers from the thousands and
thousands of potential candidates we meet throughout our lives. Although such variables as physical attractiveness and similarity of interests clearly are important in this process, the compatibility of two
people's personalities also has been a focus of much of this work. Thus,
we can ask if desire for control plays a role in who we select as our
friends and romantic partners. More generally, we can ask how important
it is for high and low desire for control people to have a lot of friends
or to spend their free time interacting with their friends. Although more
work needs to be done, the data collected thus far suggest that desire
for control may influence who we select to spend our time with, but that

high desire for control people and low desire for control people may have a different idea about the relative importance of social interactions. In addition, some research indicates that desire for control may play a role in sexual behavior.

SIMILARITY VERSUS COMPLEMENTARITY

One of the oldest issues in the social psychology of interpersonal relations concerns the question of similarity versus complementarity. Do *birds of a feather flock together* or do *opposites attract?* Are we attracted to people who share similar values, attitudes, and personality characteristics, or do complementary needs help to bind couples together? After more than three decades of research in this area there is evidence that both of these effects may operate in some relationships, perhaps at different times in the same relationship. There is much evidence that similarity often plays a role in drawing people together. There is also some, although considerably less, evidence that on occasion two people's needs will help keep them together, such as when someone with a high need to nurture is paired with someone with a high need to be taken care of.

How do individual differences in desire for control fit into this picture? On the one hand, we might predict that people of similar desire for control level will be attracted to one another. Just as with other personality variables, people probably prefer friendships and maybe romantic relationships with similar others. If you have a high desire for control, it might be difficult to understand a friend or romantic partner who did not share your belief that one should seek out leadership opportunities in a group. On the other hand, there may be a limited amount of control to go around in a relationship. If two high desire for control people both try to decide what movie the couple sees or how they structure their day, the inevitable large number of conflicts could doom the relationship. Thus, a case can be made that both similarity and complementarity will operate in the case of desire for control. What do the research data say?

The first investigation on this question provided some support for the complementarity hypothesis. These data came from an unpublished study by Schwartz, Ripley, and Conrad (1981). The researchers selected undergraduates whose DC Scale scores placed them in the upper and lower thirds of the distribution from a large sample of students. Fifteen unmarried male and fifteen unmarried female students from each group were asked to complete the DC Scale as they imagined their future marriage partner would answer the items on the scale. In other words,

TABLE 3-8. Mean Desire for Control Scores
for Self and for Ideal Marriage Partner

	Own desire for control	Ideal partner desire for control score
Males		
High desire for control subjects	116.07	102.07
Low desire for control subjects	92.13	99.80
Females		
High desire for control subjects	112.27	111.53
Low desire for control subjects	88.73	98.47

Note: From Schwartz et al. (1981)

the researchers wanted to know what kind of person the students hoped to marry someday.

The results from this study are presented in Table 3-8. As can be seen in the table, some evidence for both a complementarity and a similarity effect was uncovered. A significant interaction was found for male subjects. Both the high desire for control subjects and the subjects with a low desire for control said that they preferred a marriage partner who was considerably closer to the DC Scale mean than they were. That is, high desire for control people said that they wanted to marry someone who did not possess a high need to control events. However, male students with a low desire for control preferred to marry someone with a higher need for control than theirs.

A slightly different pattern was found for the females. Although the low desire for control females preferred someone with a significantly higher need for control than theirs, the high desire for control females wanted a partner who also had a high desire for control. Thus, whereas the low desire for control females showed the complementarity pattern, the females with a high desire for control demonstrated the similarity pattern. Although the sample size is small, the data do indicate that people at least sometimes are more attracted to (or think they would be more attracted to) someone with a different rather than similar desire for control level.

Although weak, another small bit of evidence that opposites sometimes attract when it comes to desire for control comes from the study described earlier in which pairs of friends discussed solutions to hypothetical problems. The undergraduate students in that investigation were instructed to come to the experiment with someone they considered a good same-gender friend. Although falling short of statistical significance, there was a slight tendency for people to come with a friend who was opposite of themselves in terms of need for control, $r = -.11$.

These two studies hint that if desire for control affects attraction, it may sometimes operate in a complementarity pattern. However, other research findings paint a different picture. The first evidence for this other view comes from the unpublished study in which we listened in on casual conversations. The subjects in this study were pairs of people around the university who were sitting together and carrying on a conversation that lasted for at least five minutes. When we correlated DC Scale scores for the 29 pairs of subjects we found a strong positive correlation, $r = .50$. Although the pairs of subjects in the study were not necessarily good friends, all told us that they had known one another before they had gotten together that day. Although the correlation is so high that I might not expect to find such a strong relationship in a replication of this study, the data are impressive. When people select someone to socialize with casually, they seem to choose a person with a similar desire for control.

I also looked at desire for control scores among romantically involved couples. The earlier study by Schwartz *et al.* (1981) asked students to complete the DC Scale for themselves and then for the kind of person they would probably be married to someday. There are reasons to look at the results of this study with suspicion. First, for most undergraduates marriage is a rather distant, abstract concept. We have to question whether reports on what their marriage partner would be like are based on any reasonable information or thoughtful analysis. Second, we cannot expect these subjects to understand the dynamics of how similarity and complementarity affect their choice of marriage partner. Although they may believe that an ideal partner would complement their need for control, this does not mean that they will eventually select someone who fits this description. Too many variables they are not aware of probably will direct their choice of partner and how their relationship develops. The study may simply tell us that subjects believe in the old axioms *opposites attract* and *too many chiefs* when speculating about the nature of romantic relationships.

Consequently, I asked undergraduates in another unpublished study to complete the DC Scale. Participation in the experiment was limited to students who currently were involved in an exclusive romantic relationship that had lasted for at least three months. Subjects were given a second copy of the DC Scale along with an envelope and told to ask their romantic partner to complete the scale alone and return it to the experimenter in the envelope. When I looked at the correlation between the couples' DC Scale scores, I found a significant positive correlation, $r = .33$. That is, the subjects in the sample tended to select romantic partners with a similar desire for control.

What can we conclude at this point about how desire for control affects choice of friends and romantic partners? Although much work remains, it seems fair to conclude that the strongest evidence to date suggests that desire for control affects relationships in a similarity, rather than a complementarity, pattern. It is possible that people typically hold the belief that only one person can take control of a relationship and that the ideal partner will either make decisions for you or will follow your decisions. However, a large body of research tells us that the process of meeting people, getting acquainted, developing and then maintaining a relationship is a complex matter. It does not seem impossible that two people with a high desire for control could work things out so that neither person feels frustrated in that need. Further, the data indicate that we find people of a similar desire for control level attractive. People with a high need for control may admire someone who shares this need and who acts in a similar manner. Thus, two people with a high desire for control might be attracted to one another because they both like to get involved in organizing events or in working on challenging tasks. In addition, as suggested by the research reviewed earlier, people of a similar desire for control level might be attracted to one another because they have a similar interpersonal style. Although issues remain, the evidence to date suggests that our level of desire for control, along with many other variables, may play a significant role in determining who we choose to spend our time with.

FRIENDSHIPS AND LONELINESS

Research reviewed earlier found that high desire for control people initiate fewer conversations with their friends than do people with a low desire for control and that they find these conversations less pleasant. This finding suggests that high desire for control people may be less interested in social interactions than people with a low desire for control. There are several reasons why this might be the case. First, as described earlier, social interactions might be threatening for someone who wishes to control many of the events in his or her life. There is the ever-present possibility that one will be taken advantage of or otherwise manipulated or controlled by this other person. Despite the use of some of the control-enhancing strategies uncovered in research, our ability to control social interactions is limited. In addition, we might say in a more positive manner that high desire for control people simply find many other activities that better suit their needs. As we will discover in later chapters, people with a high desire for control find more satisfaction in working on challenging tasks than do people with a low desire for control. High desire for control people are more likely to enjoy working on a hobby that provides a sense of mastery, such as painting a landscape or building a model. We might guess that the sense of understanding and accomplishment that comes with reading also would be more appealing to high desire for control people than to people with a low desire for control. In short, many of the solitary activities that one can do may provide more satisfaction for someone with a high desire for control than engaging in control-threatening social interactions.

I began to explore this question by comparing DC Scale scores with a number of measures of sociability. Seventy-five undergraduate students in this unpublished study completed a measure of need for privacy (Burger, 1989b). The scale is designed to measure the extent to which people prefer and enjoy spending time by themselves. Subjects also were asked to estimate how much of their free time (time not spent in class, at work, studying, and so on) they spent with friends. I then asked them to indicate how many people fell into the following three categories for them: close friends, good friends, and people I enjoy being with/doing things with. The questionnaire explained that a person could only be counted in one category. I also asked subjects what they considered to be the ideal number of close friends. Finally, I presented subjects with a list of six ways they might spend a free afternoon and asked them to rank in order their preferences for each activity. I included three group activities and three individual activities on the list. In order of presentation, the list was: go to the beach or a movie with a friend, pleasure reading, exercise by myself (for example, running), visit or hang out with friends, work on a hobby alone, play some group game (for example, basketball).

The scores from each of these measures were correlated with the subject's score on the DC Scale. The results are presented in Table 3-9. A fairly clear pattern emerges in these data. Although falling short of

TABLE 3-9. Correlations between DC Scale Scores
and Measures of Social Activities and Friendships

	r with DC Scale
Need for privacy scale	.12
Free time spent alone	−.14
Number of close friends	−.15*
Number of good friends	−.20**
Number of people enjoy being with/doing things with	.00
Ideal number of close friends	−.22**
Preference for individual activities	.30***

Note: * $p < .10$; ** $p < .05$; *** $p < .01$, one-tail tests

statistical significance, a high desire for control score is associated with a higher need for privacy and having spent less free time the past week with friends. More to the point, I also looked at how subjects said they would *prefer* to spend their free time. I summed subjects' preference rankings for the three individual activities on the list of ways to spend a free afternoon. These scores were significantly correlated with desire for control, with higher scores indicating a preference for the individual activities over the group activities.

I found a similar picture of high desire for control people when looking at the number of friends subjects reported having. People with a high desire for control said they have fewer close friends than do people with a low desire for control. Those in the upper third of the DC distribution reported having an average of 5.33 close friends, whereas the lowest third reported an average of 6.65 close friends. However, before assuming that this is a problem for high desire for control people, we should note that these numbers are consistent with the subjects' *preferred* number of close friends. Not only did the high desire for control subjects not have as many close friends as the subjects with a low desire for control, they did not want as many close friends. Those in the upper third of the distribution said an average of 5.84 close friends is ideal, whereas the lower third said 7.30 was the ideal number.

A high desire for control also was associated with the number of good friends. The highest third said that they had an average of 12.17 good friends, whereas the lowest-scoring DC third averaged 19.17 good friends. Interestingly, desire for control was not related to the number of people the subjects said they enjoyed spending time with.

Taken together, the data from this study clearly indicate that high desire for control people are more likely to limit their number of friends and are more likely to elect to spend their free time by themselves than are people with a low desire for control. But while these people have less social contact than do low desire for control people, the data also indicate that this does not necessarily make them less happy. Research on loneliness (cf. Hojat & Crandall, 1987; Peplau & Perlman, 1982) indicates that people feel lonely when the amount and quality of social interaction they perceive they have falls short of the amount and quality of social interaction they desire. We might conclude from this description that because high desire for control people have less of an interest in social interaction than people with a low desire for control, they may actually be less susceptible to bouts of loneliness than are low desire for control people.

A large amount of data relevant to this question has been reported by Solano (1987). She examined correlations between the DC Scale and two measures of loneliness: the UCLA Loneliness Scale (Russell, Peplau, & Cutrona, 1980) and the Differential Loneliness Scale (DLS) (Schmidt & Sermat, 1983). The UCLA scale measures a relatively stable tendency for people to experience loneliness. The DLS examines loneliness as it relates to four kinds of social deficits: friendships, family relationships, romantic/sexual relationships, and larger groups relationships. Solano collected data from undergraduates for several consecutive semesters, with more than two thousand subjects in her final sample.

The correlations Solano reports are presented in Table 3-10. As we can see from the table, there is a small but persistent negative relationship between desire for control scores and loneliness scores. This finding is consistent with the data and analysis presented earlier. Although people with a high desire for control have fewer friends, they also prefer it that way. Because social contacts are not as important to them, they are not as susceptible to loneliness as are low desire for control people who have a stronger need for social interaction.

SEXUAL BEHAVIOR

Eventually an examination of interpersonal behavior probably has to include questions about sexual behavior. Two studies have looked at the relationship between desire for control and this most intimate of social contact. One of these studies is an unpublished investigation by Gary Leak of Creighton University (Leak, 1985). During the course of examining an unrelated hypothesis, Leak collected data that allowed him to compare DC Scale scores with some measures of sexual behavior. He found a slightly positive correlation between desire for control and the number of different sexual partners people reported to have had in their lives, $r = .20$, $p < .09$. However, the scale did not correlate with a measure of the number of different sexual acts people had engaged in, $r = .07$.

TABLE 3-10. Correlations between
DC Scale and Measures of Loneliness

	Males	Females
UCLA Loneliness Scale	−.19***	−.12**
Differential Loneliness Scale		
Family	−.15**	.02
Friend	−.15**	−.04
Romantic	−.12*	−.13*
Community	−.11*	.01

Note: * $p < .01$; ** $p < .001$; *** $p < .0001$; from Solano (1987); reprinted by permission

I found a similar relationship in some unreported data I also collected while examining an unrelated hypothesis (Burger & Burns, 1988). We surveyed female undergraduates about their sexual behavior. We divided these women into those who had been sexually active during the past six months (defined as having sexual intercourse during this period) and those who were not sexually active. When we compared DC Scale scores for the two groups, we found the sexually active women tended to have a higher desire for control ($M = 105.07$) than the women who were not sexually active ($M = 99.70$), $F (1,67) = 3.30$, $p < .07$.

Because neither of these studies was designed to test a prediction about the relationship between desire for control and sexual behavior, we are now limited to some post hoc attempts to explain the results. I would also like to emphasize that, although the findings from the two studies are consistent, in both cases the relationship falls just short of statistical significance. Nonetheless, the results are tantalizing enough to provoke some speculation about how desire for control might be related to frequency of sexual behavior. My best guess at this point is that high desire for control people are more likely than people with a low desire for control to take charge of every aspect of their lives, including their sexual lives. Thus, the college women with a high desire for control in the Burger and Burns (1988) study may have been more assertive about exploring and expressing their sexual interests than the students with a low desire for control.

Although the reasons behind the relationship between desire for control and frequency of sexual activity remain fuzzy, a clear prediction can be made about the relationship between desire for control and use of contraception. Many psychologists and community workers have been puzzled about the too-common failure of sexually active teenagers and college students to use reliable and readily available methods of contraception. Currently three million American women a year experience an unwanted pregnancy. Half of these pregnancies end in abortion.

Why do so many people risk an unwanted pregnancy when simple and inexpensive means of prevention are available? Researchers have found many variables that contribute to this phenomenon. I can speculate that one of the variables determining whether sexually active people use contraception might be the person's desire for control level. For most unmarried people, particularly college students, an unwanted pregnancy is something to be avoided. Although many of these people apparently are content to leave their chances of an unwanted pregnancy to fate, others are motivated to take action to keep themselves from falling victim to this misfortune. It seems reasonable to predict that people with a high desire for control would be less likely than people with a low desire for control to leave such an important consequence to chance. Rather, their need to control events should lead them to take actions to control to a large degree whether or not they or their partner becomes pregnant.

I examined this prediction as part of the survey of female college students described above (Burger & Burns, 1988). This previously unreported analysis supported the prediction. Desire for Control Scale scores correlated significantly with the percentage of time students reported using contraception when they engaged in sexual intercourse, $r = .22$, $p < .05$. The higher the student's desire for control, the more likely she was to use contraception. Interestingly, Leak (1985) found that desire for control was not related to a scale assessing knowledge about contraception, $r = -.09$. Thus, although both high desire for control college students and low desire for control students may know about contraception, the students with a high desire are more likely to do something to control their chances of becoming involved in an unwanted pregnancy.

SUMMARY

The many studies reported in this chapter indicate that individual differences in desire for control play a significant role in how we interact with others. The research to date indicates that high desire for control people and low desire for control people differ in their interaction style, how much they enjoy social interactions, and whom they choose to interact with. But the collection of findings also reminds us that any behavior as complex as social interaction is influenced by an uncountable number of variables. Simple statements about how desire for control affects social behavior are easy to make, but difficult to support unequivocally with research data. We have uncovered seemingly inconsistent findings at several points in this work. For example, no clear pattern has been found when looking at whether high desire for control people use certain control-enhancing behaviors, whether these people speak up or wait to talk, or whether people prefer romantic partners with a similar or dissimilar desire for control. Nonetheless, that these and other social behaviors are related to desire for control seems fairly certain. Social interactions and interpersonal relations play an important and pervasive part of our lives, and problems in these areas typically lead to psychological distress. Thus, untangling the role of desire for control in this process remains a challenging, but worthy, pursuit.

CHAPTER 4

SOCIAL INFLUENCE

With or without our awareness, intentionally or incidentally, one of the consequences of social interaction is that we often influence the behavior of the people we come into contact with. The question of social influence has been central to social psychology since Triplett (1898) conducted what is widely recognized as the first social psychology experiment. Triplett studied bicycle racers to determine why racers tended to perform better in the presence of other competitors than when alone. Decades of subsequent research has examined social influence from a number of perspectives. We know that people often behave very differently in groups than they do when alone, that people conform to social norms even without being aware they are doing so, and that under certain circumstances it is possible to change a listener's attitude with a well-crafted persuasive message. In short, people influence one another.

What all of these social influence effects have in common is that one or more persons are, in effect, *controlling* the behavior of another person. If this is the case, then we can ask a number of questions relevant to individual differences in desire for control. For example, are some people more likely to attempt to influence others' behavior? Are some people more susceptible or resistant to social influence? Do people differ in the extent to which they are successful at social influence? Do some people resent depending on help from others or relying on other people? Are some influence strategies more or less successful depending upon the audience?

We can begin to answer these questions by noting that high desire for control people want to perceive themselves as being in control of what happens to them. Consequently, they should be less likely than low desire for control people to be satisfied with a situation in which someone else tells them what to do. Accurately or not, high desire for control people are motivated to believe that they make their own decisions and are not subject to control by salespeople, speakers, or group pressures. We also should expect that high desire for control people are probably more likely than people with a low desire for control to want to influence the actions of those around them. They prefer to give directions than follow them. Therefore, as a general guideline for understanding the role of desire for control in social influence situations, we can say that high desire for control people are more resistant than low desire for control people to efforts to control their behavior, but that they are more likely to try to change the actions of others.

The research to date examining the effects of desire for control in social influence situations tends to support the above reasoning. Compared to people with a low desire for control, high desire for control people are more likely to take action to influence others, to resist direct and indirect conformity pressures, to react negatively to behavior that challenges their sense of self-determination, and to experience greater feeling of crowdedness and discomfort in a high-density environment.

INFLUENCING THE BEHAVIOR OF OTHERS

Sometimes the need to control the events in their lives requires high desire for control people to exercise control over aspects of other people's lives as well. Many of the important events in our lives take place in social situations. For most people, controlling what happens at work means influencing colleagues, customers, and bosses effectively. Most people belong to social, political, or other types of organizations. Some members are content to go along with the group's wishes, others prefer to have a say in what those wishes are. We would expect, therefore, that high desire for control people will more often engage in efforts to influence the actions of others than will people with a low desire for control. Indeed, one of the factors that seems to make up the desire for control construct has to do with taking on leadership roles in group settings (see Chapter 2).

We would expect further that high desire for control people are more likely than low desire for control people to get involved in community projects and efforts to make social or political changes. A person with a low desire for control might be content to allow others to make laws or to accept that community problems either cannot be changed or are not worth the effort. People with a high desire for control should show the opposite reaction. They not only want social and political changes (although not all high desire for control people share similar views on what these changes should be), they prefer to be the ones influencing decisions rather than responding to the decisions of others.

I first examined this hypothesis by asking undergraduates about their experiences with leadership roles in various clubs and organizations. I reasoned that high desire for control people could not be content to leave the decision making up to others. In most organizations, the best opportunity for influencing the activities of the entire group comes from serving as one of the officers. Indeed, we sometimes hear people complain about a power-hungry club president who tries to exert too much control over the membership.

I asked 98 undergraduates in an unpublished study to indicate if they currently or in the past few years had held an officer's role in any of the following types of organizations: student government, campus organization, religious organization, political organization, hobby/sports organization, or any other category of club or organization. I totaled the number of different organizations for which subjects indicated they currently or recently held a leadership role to form an overall leadership score. This score was positively correlated with the DC Scale score, $r = .24$ ($p < .05$). Further analyses found that the correlation was slightly higher for females, $r = .28$ ($p < .05$) than for males, $r = .18$. Although the leadership measure was crude, the data are consistent with the prediction that high desire for control people are more likely to take on active efforts to influence others than are people with a low desire for control.

Zimmerman (1990; Zimmerman & Rappaport, 1988) examined the relationship between desire for control and participation in community action in a more elaborate set of studies. In one laboratory experiment, undergraduates were presented with some hypothetical community issues (for example, closing a neighborhood school) and asked to estimate the extent to which they would be willing to try to change the situation (Zimmerman & Rappaport, 1988). Although we must be cautious in placing too much credence on what college students say they would probably do in a very hypothetical situation, the results were informative. As expected, the more involved students said they would become in these issues, the higher their desire for control. Thus, because they prefer to influence events in their community rather than sit by and let them happen, high desire for control subjects were more likely than subjects with a low desire for control to want to do what they could to change a situation they did not like.

The researchers provided more convincing evidence for this conclusion in two additional experiments, one with an undergraduate population and one with a sample from the community at large (Zimmerman

& Rappaport, 1988). Subjects indicated which community activities on a predetermined list they had participated in during the past year. The activities examined were those suggesting that the participant was making an effort to influence public policy in some way. The activities ranged from voting and signing a petition to writing letters to government officials and working on political campaigns. Further, subjects were asked to indicate the extent to which they were involved in the organizations they belonged to. That is, subjects listed some groups they belonged to (for example, service organizations, hobby groups, church groups) and the extent to which they attended meetings, volunteered their time, held leadership positions, and so on.

A very consistent pattern emerged on these measures with both the student and community samples. More participation in community activities, as indicated by number of activities and level of involvement, was significantly associated with higher levels of desire for control. The studies are particularly impressive because they demonstrate that high desire for control people not only express a stronger desire than low desire for control people to do something about influencing community events and policies, but also are more likely to get involved and take actions to exercise that control.

Reed (1989) studied a more specific application of this phenomenon. He was interested in the question of whether the personality characteristics of union organizers had an effect on the success or failure of union representation elections. Reed identified several personality trait scales that theoretically might predict effective union organizing. The list included a measure of locus of control and the DC Scale. The union organizer's job is clearly one that provides a sense of leadership and influence over an important aspect of a union member's life. We would expect that such a position would be particularly attractive to someone with a high desire for control. Further, as Reed predicted, we would also expect that the higher the organizers' desire for control, the more effort they would put into the job and the more likely they would be to succeed.

One of the most striking aspects of the findings from this research is that the 64 union organizers who participated in the study had an average DC Scale score of 113.51, more than a standard deviation above the mean usually found in this age group. This suggests that high desire for control union members are more likely than union members with a low desire for control to aspire to and attain the role of union organizer. In addition, Reed found that desire for control was one of the personality variables that consistently predicted success at union organizing. The higher the desire for control, the more likely the organizer would succeed. It is interesting to note that locus of control showed the opposite relationship predicted by Reed. Organizers with an external locus of control were more successful in their organization efforts than those with an internal locus of control.

In summary, research using various populations suggests that high desire for control people are more likely than low desire for control people to take on roles and get involved in activities and organizations. It is fairly clear in each of the examples studied that exercising influence over these other people also helped the high desire for control people to exercise control over some important events in their own lives. Thus, these data do not tell us whether people with a high desire for control have a need to influence others generally. For example, high desire for control people might just as well prefer that someone else take over organizing a dance or fundraiser, if they have little interest in how that activity turns out.

REACTION TO PERSUASIVE EFFORTS AND CONFORMITY PRESSURES

If high desire for control people are motivated to see themselves in control of what they do and when they do it, they should be more resistant than low desire for control people when someone tries to exert influence over them. Sometimes these influence attempts come in the form of direct, calculated tactics, such as a salesperson trying to sell a product to a customer. But other times we conform to less obvious social pressures, such as when we change our tastes in clothing or music in a way that just happens to resemble the tastes of the people we work with. In either case, we would expect low desire for control people to be more susceptible to influence pressures than people with a high desire for control.

REACTION TO DIRECT PERSUASIVE EFFORTS

Telling someone that "you must buy this product" or "you have no choice but to agree" is not likely to alter the attitudes or behavior of high desire for control people. These people want to maintain the perception that they buy their products, develop their attitudes, and vote for their candidates because they freely choose to do so, not because they succumb to pressure. Although high desire for control people are not immune to a good sales pitch, we would expect them to typically put up more resistance than low desire for control people to direct persuasive efforts that challenge their sense of self-determination.

   This line of reasoning is tied directly to the pioneering work of Jack Brehm (1966; Brehm & Brehm, 1981) on *reactance theory*. According to Brehm, we are all motivated to some extent to see ourselves as having freedom of choice. When that freedom to act and choose as we please is threatened, we react. Typically this reaction means taking actions to reassert our ability to make our own choices. Thus, people who are told that they have no option but to go along with a speaker's position often react by changing their attitude in the direction opposite of that advocated by the speaker. Shoppers pressured to purchase a particular brand may be less likely to buy the product than those shoppers who feel they are free to choose whatever brand they want. Reacting against direct pressure helps us maintain the sense that we are in control of our actions and attitudes.

   If we apply individual differences in desire for control to reactance theory, a fairly straightforward prediction emerges. High desire for control people should have a stronger reaction to perceived threats to their freedom of choice than those people with a low desire for control. Consequently, we would expect that people with a high desire for control would show a larger reactance effect to direct pressure to change their views than would low desire for control people. Although the prediction is clear, I must admit that so far two attempts to demonstrate this effect empirically have failed. A third attempt with a more refined methodology may be coming some day, but in the meantime evidence from other sources supports the hypothesis that high desire for control people react differently than low desire for control people to direct efforts to influence their behavior or change their attitudes.

   One study that supports this position was conducted by Burger and Vartabedian (1980). We reasoned that people with a high desire for control would be most resistant to a persuasive speech when they initially disagreed with the speaker's position. These people are motivated to believe that their attitudes are the result of their own reasoning and logic, rather than a reaction to a speaker. Thus, high desire for control people should be reluctant to accept the arguments of someone presenting an opposing viewpoint. To do otherwise would be an admission that one changed his or her attitude as a result of hearing the speech. On the other hand, this resistance might not be present when listening to the arguments of a speaker who shares the general viewpoint of the high desire for control person. Because they are less threatening, high desire for control people might listen to these arguments, and perhaps change their attitude to be more in line with that advocated by the speaker. We might further speculate that low desire for control people, not burdened with this strong need to feel in control of their opinions, might be more persuaded by the counterattitudinal arguments, which they probably have not considered or been exposed to before.

We tested this reasoning with students in introductory communication classes. The students completed a questionnaire during class asking them to indicate their positions on a number of political and social issues through the use of nine-point scales. They also completed the DC Scale. From their responses we determined that the issue that best created a bimodal distribution of attitudes was the Equal Rights Amendment (ERA). That is, very few students indicated a midpoint opinion on this question. They tended to support or not support the adoption of the ERA.

Three weeks later the class instructor asked students to read a speech, supposedly written by a graduate student, as part of a class exercise. No connection was made with the earlier data collection. Two speeches were randomly distributed, one that advocated a pro-ERA position, and one that argued against adoption of the amendment. After reading the speech, subjects were asked to evaluate the speech and speech writer on a number of dimensions, and were asked to give their own position on the ERA on a nine-point scale item worded identically to the one they had answered three weeks earlier.

We compared subjects' stated positions on the ERA after reading the speech to the positions they had given earlier. We also divided subjects into those who had heard a speech consistent with their initial view and those who had heard a counterattitudinal message. As expected, high desire for control subjects were more likely to be persuaded by the speech when they initially agreed with the speaker's position than when they read a speech with which they disagreed. Half of the high desire for control subjects changed their position more toward the pole advocated by the speaker when they were already leaning that way. However, only 31% moved in the speaker's direction when they initially disagreed with the advocated position. The subjects with a low desire for control showed the opposite pattern. Only 20% changed in the direction advocated in the speech when they initially agreed with the speaker, as compared with 65% who were persuaded by the speech with which they initially disagreed.

These findings suggest that high desire for control people react more strongly to efforts to change their attitudes than do people with a low desire for control. One way they deal with these efforts is to resist the advocated position, perhaps by arguing against the points raised by the speaker or by simply dismissing the advocate's credibility. Although much more work needs to be done in this area, evidence from this study and some research reviewed in the next section support the notion that high desire for control people are more likely to show a reactance effort than low desire for control people.

REACTION TO CONFORMITY PRESSURE

We encounter direct efforts to change our attitudes and behaviors daily. But social psychologists have long been interested in the ways our attitudes are shaped by the people around us in ways we may not be aware of. Perhaps the most influential of the research paradigms in this area was developed by Solomon Asch (1951) to study conformity effects. Subjects in this classic set of experiments were shown a line and asked simply to judge which line from a group of three was the same length as the first line. The task is so easy that virtually everyone with normal vision gets the answer correct every time. However, subjects in some conditions first heard several other subjects (really experimental confederates) give incorrect answers. These subjects often reacted by giving the same answer as the confederates. Of particular interest were the subjects who convinced themselves that they actually saw what the confederates said was the right answer.

The Asch studies and the many subsequent experiments using this paradigm have intrigued psychologists for the past four decades. Perhaps the reason for this interest lies in what the studies suggest about the way we all conform to perceived norms. If a significant number of subjects can change the way they see a set of lines simply by learning that a few other people see things that way, what does this say about our tendency to conform to tastes in clothing, music, and political attitudes?

It should be evident that none of us easily or ever escapes the influence of such conformity pressures. However, it may very well be the case that people are more or less susceptible to conformity pressures depending on their level of desire for control. That is, we would expect that high desire for control people would be less likely than low desire for control people to conform to a perceived norm. These people have developed a style of deciding things for themselves, rather than relying on others' advice or direction. In fact, the argument that everyone does it may result in a type of reactance effect for high desire for control people, who prefer to believe that they make up their own minds. On the other hand, low desire for control people not only lack this need to see their judgments as uninfluenced by others, but may prefer to go along with the norm and avoid the problems of standing out from the crowd.

I tested this hypothesis in three experiments (Burger, 1987a). In the first experiment undergraduate subjects read what they believed to be an editorial written by an executive of the National Collegiate Athletic Association (NCAA). The writer discussed some of the problems of college athletes, then proposed a change in NCAA policy that allowed athletes to play on college teams without having to take classes. Half of the subjects read a version of the editorial in which the writer presents the results of a survey showing strong support among college students for the points he made and for enacting the proposed plan. For example, subjects read that 73% of those surveyed said that they would like to see the plan enacted. Information about the survey was not included in the editorial for the other half.

Subjects responded to several questionnaire items to indicate the extent to which they agreed with the editorial writer's opinion. Low desire for control subjects responded to the survey data as expected. They were more likely to agree with the writer's position when they had read that the majority of people felt this way than when they did not receive this information. However, the reaction of the subjects with a high desire for control was particularly interesting. Not only were they not persuaded by the survey results, they were actually *less* likely to agree with the speaker after hearing that this position was the majority opinion than when not reading about the survey. These high desire for control subjects seemed to react to the norm information with a type of reactance effect. They appeared to interpret the survey results as pressure to agree with the writer. It was as if the writer were saying, "nearly everyone agrees with me, so you must also." As a result, these high desire for control subjects established their sense of self-determination about the issue by taking a stand different from that advocated by the writer. Although this effect was not predicted, it may well be the reactance effect I have been unable to obtain in previous studies designed specifically to elicit just such an effect.

A second experiment examined the effects of desire for control on conformity using procedures similar to the original Asch paradigm. Instead of using line-length judgments, which undergraduates may have read about in high school or college psychology courses, we used humor judgments. Through pilot testing we selected ten cartoons from newspapers that college students agreed were not very funny. As in the Asch studies, three student confederates, posing as subjects, participated in the experiment along with the real subjects in the conformity conditions. The cartoons were presented on slides and subjects were asked to indicate how funny they found the cartoon on a 100-point scale, with 100 being the highest. The experimenter explained that he wanted the subjects to give their immediate reaction out loud, but that because not everyone could speak up at once, subjects would draw slips to determine the order in which they gave their responses. Naturally, the drawing was rigged so that the real subject always went last. The three confederates gave predetermined responses indicating that the cartoons were fairly amusing, with an average rating of about 70. They also occasionally laughed, smirked, or giggled at the cartoons. A control condition also was created in which subjects rated the cartoons in the absence of the confederates.

The results were as expected, with the exception that even without norm information subjects generally found the cartoons to be much funnier than we had originally thought. In the absence of other "subjects," high desire for control subjects rated the cartoons as slightly funnier ($M = 49.3$) than did the subjects with a low desire for control ($M = 43.7$). However, when they first heard the three confederates indicate that the cartoons were particularly funny, the low desire for control subjects said that they found the cartoons funnier ($M = 73.2$) than did the subjects with a high desire for control ($M = 62.1$). Although clearly both conformed to the norm pressure and rated the cartoons funnier, the low desire for control subjects were more likely to do this than the high desire for control subjects. In fact, the low desire for control subjects actually rated the cartoons on average as slightly funnier than the confederates had.

The results are entirely consistent with the description of high desire for control people as less susceptible to conformity pressure than people with a low desire for control. Unfortunately, the procedures allow for an alternative interpretation of the findings. It is possible that subjects in the conformity conditions were reacting to the mere presence of the other people in the room rather than to the ratings they gave to the cartoons. It is possible that the presence of others listening to the subjects' evaluations created increased arousal, which has been found in other studies to increase how funny people find humorous situations.

Consequently, we conducted another experiment which replicated the first one exactly, except that we also added a condition in which subjects heard the confederates rate the same ten cartoons as particularly unfunny. Subjects in this condition heard the confederates give responses that averaged approximately 20 on the 100-point scale. The results of the experiment are presented in Table 4-1. Both high and low desire for control subjects conformed to the group norm in both the funny and not-funny conditions. However, as expected, the high desire for control subjects were less likely to conform in either direction.

In summary, the research to date indicates clearly that high desire for control people and people with a low desire for control react differently to direct and less obvious pressures to conform. It is simply more

TABLE 4-1. Mean Humor Scores for Ten Cartoons

Condition	High desire for control subjects	Low desire for control subjects
Confederates rate cartoons funny	64.8	70.8
No confederates	49.0	46.3
Confederates rate cartoons not funny	27.8	20.5

Note: From Burger (1987a); copyright © 1987 by the American Psychological Association; reprinted by permission of the publisher

difficult to influence a person with a high desire for control than someone with a low desire for control. Of course, as shown in the humor judgment studies, high desire for control people do conform, but not as much as the people with a low desire for control. This desire to see themselves as the shapers of their own attitudes can even lead high desire for control people to sometimes react against an advocated position, as demonstrated in the NCAA editorial experiment. In either case, the high desire for control people are attempting to maintain the perception that they make up their own minds, and that they resent attempts by other people to tell them what it is they ought to be doing or thinking.

THREATS TO CONTROL IN EVERYDAY INTERACTIONS

Threats to perceived control are not limited to direct persuasive efforts or less obvious conformity pressure. As described in Chapter 3, interacting with others often involves issues relevant to a need for control. Sometimes people inadvertently threaten our perception of personal control. For example, while offering assistance to another person may seem like an entirely positive and altruistic thing to do, some research finds that the person receiving the help does not always see it that way. Being on the receiving end of helping behavior may challenge people's perceptions that they are able to look out for themselves. Receiving may make some people feel dependent and lacking control over some important aspect of their lives (Nadler, 1986; Nadler & Fisher, 1986). This section will look at three examples illustrating that because interacting with others typically has implications for control, high desire for control people and people with a low desire for control may have very different reactions to another person's behavior.

The first example of this phenomenon deals with how people react to receiving help from others. Investigators find that recipients sometimes react with increased distress or that they simply prefer that the help-giver not provide assistance. One explanation for this effect is that the help recipient may experience a blow to his or her self-esteem, particularly if the help-giver is of similar status to the recipient and if the assistance is in an area that is central to the recipient's sense of self. Thus, a student who prides herself on her math ability is likely to resent help on a math homework assignment from one of her classmates. However, if she freely admits to not knowing how to roller-skate, then help from a professional skater is likely to be welcome.

Although the self-esteem explanation makes sense and there is some evidence to support this interpretation, an alternative explanation based on the notion of desire for control can also be introduced. Nadler and Fisher (1986) argue that at times receiving help can lead to the perception that one has lost control. If that is the case, then we would expect people who typically are highly motivated to see themselves in control to show stronger negative reactions to receiving help than those less motivated to see themselves in control.

Evidence in support of this position comes from some unpublished research by Kim Daubman of Williams College. Daubman (1990) examined individual differences in desire for control as well as self-esteem in the typical experimental paradigm used to examine recipient reactions to help. Pairs of undergraduates worked independently on a set of puzzles. False feedback indicated that the subject had done only about average, while the other subjects had done quite well on the first set of puzzles. Subjects then either did or did not receive a helpful hint from the other subject on how to solve the problems.

Daubman looked at a number of reactions to this experience. She found, as predicted, that whereas low desire for control subjects generally felt better after receiving the help, the subjects with a high desire for control felt worse. Further, whereas receiving help tended to lower slightly the motivation of the low desire for control subjects to perform well on the next task, the opposite was the case for the high desire for control subjects. High desire for control subjects who received help reported that it was more important for them to do well and spent more time working on the task than high desire for control subjects who did not receive help. It is especially notable that the latter finding occurred only in conditions in which subjects expected immediate feedback on their performance. In addition, half of the high desire for control subjects said that receiving help was irritating, whereas only 22.7% of the subjects with a low desire for control admitted feeling this way.

Thus, Daubman's data suggest strongly that high desire for control people are more likely than low desire for control people to interpret assistance from another person as a threat to their ability to control the situation themselves. As a result, these high desire for control people are likely to resent the help-giver's gesture and may then react by working all the harder to demonstrate that they can overcome the challenge on their own without anyone's help. Daubman further argues that past research finding a link between individual differences in self-esteem and reactions to receiving help failed to recognize that self-esteem is correlated with desire for control (see Chapter 7). Consequently, it is difficult to know if the individual differences effects uncovered in that research were due to self-esteem or desire for control. Nonetheless, the findings may explain why some high desire for control people I know resist asking for directions and instead will drive around unnecessarily trying desperately to demonstrate their mastery over the task of getting from point A to point B.

A second example of how high desire for control people sometimes interpret the behavior of others in control-threatening ways concerns how we respond when other people violate our expectations for their behavior. Schönbach (1990) calls such incidents *account episodes,* and argues that such violations threaten our perception that we can control our social interactions. That is, we have learned to expect certain standards of behavior from the people we interact with. If someone accidentally spills coffee on us, we expect an apology and efforts to correct the situation. Because our behavior and the behavior of most people is governed by a host of social rules most of the time, we come to depend on other people to act in these predictable ways.

However, sometimes we encounter people who do something wrong, and then fail to rectify the situation in the predictable manner prescribed by social norms. To use one of Schönbach's experimental vignettes, suppose your babysitter had failed to keep an eye on your child and the child had hurt himself or herself. In a predictable, controllable world the babysitter would immediately apologize for his or her failure and try to rectify the situation by perhaps paying for the child's medical bills or offering free babysitting services in the future. But how might you react if the babysitter did not show appropriate remorse?

Schönbach (1990) provides data from five separate studies indicating that high desire for control people have a more difficult time accepting this situation and respond more strongly than do people with a low desire for control. Further, Schönbach (1990) provides evidence that when given information that things are set on the right path again, such as when the violator makes amends, high desire for control people are more likely to respond positively to this turn of events. This research demonstrates once again that high desire for control people have a need to control the behavior of others. This need to influence others is likely to surface when the other person's behavior affects the level of perceived control over important events of the high desire for control person.

Finally, sometimes high desire for control people react to others in a control-threatened manner even when just reading about or hearing about what happens to other people. Much research finds that people often derogate the victims of crimes and accidents (Lerner & Miller, 1978). That is, we often view the victims of such misfortunes as bad people or otherwise deserving of their fate. One explanation for this effect is that people are motivated to maintain a belief that the world is a just place, where good things happen to good people and unfortunate events happen to bad people. Indeed, ample evidence supports this *just world hypothesis*.

But why do people have a strong need to believe that the world is a fair and just place? As explained by Lerner and Miller (1978), we need to believe that there is a way to avoid calamities and misfortunes. If we accept the idea that terrible misfortunes can happen to anyone at anytime, we render ourselves vulnerable. However, if we can interpret accounts of tragedies so that we maintain the belief that such events do not happen in a random, haphazard way, we are able to say to ourselves that whether we will fall victim to such a misfortune is to some extent under our control.

Feinberg, Powell, and Miller (1982) hypothesized from this reasoning that the greater an individual's desire for control, the more he or she would engage in victim derogation to maintain the sense of control over such events. To test this hypothesis, undergraduate females were administered the DC Scale and the Just World Scale (Rubin & Peplau, 1975). The Just World Scale was designed to measure the extent to which test takers generally believe that people tend to get what they deserve and deserve what they get. As expected, a strong positive correlation was found between the measures, $r = .50$. That is, the higher a subject's desire for control, the more she tended to believe that the world was a just and fair place.

Taken together, the three examples described above provide additional evidence for the notion that desire for control affects the way we react to the behavior of other people, even in situations that do not at first appear relevant to a need for control. Because other people often behave in ways that threaten our sense of personal control, high desire for control people are more likely to feel threatened and react more strongly to rectify these situations than are low desire for control people. This threat can come from something as seemingly innocent as offering help. In the next section I take this reasoning one step further—

sometimes the mere presence of other people affects our sense of personal control and leads to different reactions by high desire for control people and low desire for control people.

THE PERCEPTION OF CROWDING

When concern for crowding and overpopulation became an important social and political issue in the late 1960s, many social psychologists and environmental psychologists began looking at the conditions under which people feel crowded and uncomfortable. One of the key findings from this early work was that the experience of crowding was not necessarily related to density, that is, not related to the number of people per square foot (Stokols, 1972). Some researchers found that a large number of people in a relatively small space failed to produce feelings of crowding. Although subsequent research has identified many variables that affect the perception of crowding, one of the most important is the perception of personal control. Several investigations found that people experience more discomfort and feel more crowded when too many people interfere with their ability to effectively do what they want to do in that space. In other words, high density results in the perception of being crowded when it threatens a person's sense of personal control (Schmidt & Keating, 1979). For example, if I am reading at a desk and have adequate space for this task, then it probably does not matter that the room is full. However, if I am frustrated in my efforts to move my shopping cart through the aisles of a crowded supermarket, then I may feel quite crowded. In support of this interpretation, researchers have found that one way to lower feelings of discomfort and crowding in a room with a lot of people is to give the occupants an opportunity to exercise some control over the events in that room (Rodin, Solomon, & Metcalf, 1978).

If a feeling of crowding results from a perception that our ability to exercise control over the situation is impaired, then we would expect high desire for control people to be more susceptible than low desire for control people to the experience of crowding. People with a high desire for control probably respond more quickly to even small interferences with their attempts to do something in crowded quarters. We might guess that high desire for control people avoid crowded stores and cramped offices, and that when they cannot avoid these places, they are easily annoyed when trying to work around other customers' shopping carts or officemates' equipment.

To test this idea, we asked undergraduate males to work on a series of puzzles while in a relatively small space (Burger, Oakman, & Bullard, 1983). In some conditions three subjects worked in a room 6 feet by 6 feet for 20 minutes, whereas in other conditions six subjects worked in the same room for the same length of time. We designed the puzzle task so that the higher the density the more difficult time the subjects would have completing their task. The task required subjects to come up with a numerical answer to questions such as "The year Columbus discovered America minus the number of pints in 16 fluid ounces divided by the square root of 49." Depending upon the answer, subjects then went to one of seven envelopes taped on the walls of the room for their next problem. The envelopes were arranged so that getting to the correct envelope, and indeed finding space for working on the problem, was more difficult the more bodies there were in the room. Because the subjects solved and then had to move on to their next problem in less than a minute, we expected that the high density room would lead to feelings of crowding and discomfort, especially for the high desire for control subjects.

Following this experience, subjects completed questionnaires asking about their feelings of crowdedness and discomfort. Subjects also were divided into halves according to desire for control based on test scores taken a few weeks earlier. As shown in Table 4-2, the high desire for control subjects reported feeling more crowded and less comfortable than the low desire for control subjects. Further, this difference was found in both the three-person and six-person groups. It seems that the other people in the room interfered sufficiently with the ability of the high desire for control subjects to complete the experimental task so as to create feelings of discomfort even when there were only two other people in the small room.

TABLE 4-2. Mean Crowding and Discomfort Ratings

	Six-person room		Three-person room	
	High desire for control	Low desire for control	High desire for control	Low desire for control
Crowding rating	6.19	4.85	4.47	3.55
Discomfort rating	5.56	4.22	3.95	3.24

Note: Ratings on nine-point scales, with higher scores indicating more crowding and more discomfort; from Burger et al. (1983); copyright © 1983 by The Society for Personality and Social Psychology; reprinted by permission of Sage Publications

SUMMARY

Unlike many of the topics explored in this book, the research tying desire for control to social influence has thus far produced very few surprises. I predicted rather straightforwardly from the description of desire for control that high desire for control people would be more likely than people with a low desire for control to engage in social influence and to react negatively and resist perceived threats to their personal control by others. The research findings suggest that high desire for control people are much more likely to interpret another person's actions in terms of control and to see the behavior as a threat to their ability to control the events in their own lives. Thus, while we should not be surprised to find high desire for control people reacting to direct efforts to change their attitudes, these people also seem more likely to interpret relatively innocent actions, such as offering assistance, as a threat to their self-determination. This research paints a picture of a high desire for control person constantly on guard to avoid relinquishing control of any aspect of his or her life to others if it can be helped.

One of the issues alluded to at several points in this research is whether high desire for control people prefer to control the behavior of other people generally or whether they limit their efforts to those situations that affect them directly. For example, we all know someone who seems interested in running other people's lives. Does this reflect a high desire for control? Although I am aware of no research on this question to date, I would speculate that high desire for control people probably are not interested in influencing other people's behavior *per se*. Rather, what other people do is of interest to them when their own need for control is threatened. Indeed, trying to get other people to act the way you want them to is probably difficult, frustrating work. With all of the things high desire for control people are concerned about controlling, it is difficult to see why they would waste their time with the lives of others. Indeed, worrying about what other people do probably would take away from their ability to attend to and control the important things in their own lives.

CHAPTER 5

ACHIEVEMENT BEHAVIOR AND INTRINSIC MOTIVATION

For several decades now, achievement and achievement motivation have been central topics in personality and social psychology. Every textbook covers the topic and every graduate student is familiar with some of the classic work in this area. Some psychologists have argued that this fascination with achievement is testament to the central role achievement plays in the American lifestyle. Others have credited the stimulating groundbreaking work of Henry Murray and David McClelland. Whatever the reason, research on achievement-related behavior has a long and rich history.

When reading some of this work, it soon becomes clear that the investigators often implicitly, and sometimes explicitly, touch on issues related to personal control. In particular, researchers and theorists have addressed the relationship between achievement motivation and a need to demonstrate mastery and competence (Deci, 1975; White, 1959). As described in Chapter 1, desire for control is closely related to such needs. When we divide achievement behavior into a sequence of steps, predictions can be made about differences between high desire for control people and low desire for control people at nearly every step. Many of these predictions have been supported by research findings, and a few have not. Nonetheless, what will be clear from reviewing the research reported in this chapter is that desire for control plays a significant role in achievement behavior.

A FOUR-STEP MODEL FOR DESIRE
FOR CONTROL AND ACHIEVEMENT BEHAVIOR

I began research on the relationship between desire for control and achievement behavior by outlining four steps in the achievement process that seemed relevant to individual differences in desire for control (Burger, 1985). That model is shown in Table 5-1. I did not begin with the assumption that either a high desire for control or a low desire for control would necessarily lead to higher levels of achievement. Rather, as shown in Table 5-1, there were theoretical reasons to expect that whether a high desire for control was an asset or a liability would be a function of situational variables. Nonetheless, I probably did expect that high desire for control people would achieve more in most achievement situations. I held this expectation because the characteristics that seemed to describe the way a high desire for control person would approach an achievement task—high aspiration, high effort, persistence—typically leads to success. But before addressing the question of who achieves more, let us review research associated with each step of the model.

ASPIRATION LEVEL

The first prediction I made for the relationship between desire for control and achievement was that high desire for control people would tend to set their aspiration levels higher than people with a low desire for control. High desire for control people should see an achievement

TABLE 5-1. Desire for Control—Achievement Model

	Aspiration level	Response to challenge	Persistence	Attributions for success and failure
Theoretical relationship with high DC as compared with low DC	Select harder tasks; set goals more realistically	React with greater effort	Work at difficult task longer	More likely to attribute success to self and failure to unstable source
High desire for control benefit	Higher goals are achieved	Difficult tasks are completed	Difficult tasks are completed	Motivation level remains high
High desire for control liability	May attempt goals too difficult	May develop performance-inhibiting reactions	May invest too much effort	May develop an illusion of control

Note: From Burger (1985); copyright © 1985 by the American Psychological Association; reprinted by permission of the publisher

situation as an opportunity to demonstrate their mastery and control over events. Accomplishing slightly challenging tasks can satisfy the need to feel in control that characterizes the person with a high desire for control. On the other hand, settling for lower standards or doing no better than anyone else on an achievement task might be seen as a challenge to that person's need to feel masterful.

People with high aspirations obviously have an advantage in that they are more likely to achieve these lofty goals than people who never make the effort. However, there is also the potential disadvantage of not knowing one's limits, of setting unrealistic aspiration levels that lead to an inefficient expenditure of effort and resources. People with exceptionally high aspirations may be left disappointed and distressed at having reached a level of success that still falls below their initial goal.

However, some of this disappointment can be avoided if high desire for control people are able to reassess the situation and set more realistic goals after some feedback on their initial efforts. If it becomes apparent that making straight As is not possible, then a sense of mastery might still be attained by setting one's sights on a B+ average. But are high desire for control people or low desire for control people more realistic in adjusting their aspiration levels when they discover that their initial goals were set unrealistically high? We might predict that high desire for control people would be less able to make these realistic adjustments because to do so would be to admit to their limitations. However, one could also argue that high desire for control people pay more attention to feedback and consequently alter their goals so as to maximize their achievements.

I conducted two laboratory experiments to test this step in the model (Burger, 1985). Subjects in the first experiment worked on sets of anagrams. Subjects were administered four lists of 10 relatively easy four-letter anagrams in the first part of this experiment. They were given two minutes to work on each of the four sets of anagrams, and most had little difficulty with this part of the task. Subjects then turned to the last page of the task booklet, where they were to select the anagram lists they would work on during the second half of the experiment. Subjects were instructed to select three lists from the nine lists presented on the page. The key information was the percentage of students who supposedly had been able to solve all of the anagrams on the list during earlier pilot testing. Subjects read that the most difficult list had been solved by only 10% of the subjects, whereas the easiest list had been solved by 90%. The other seven lists were presented with increments of 10% success rates, thus providing a nine-point scale of difficulty.

As expected, although the high desire for control subjects and the low desire for control subjects had performed nearly identically on the first four sets of anagrams, high desire for control subjects selected more challenging tasks for the second part of the experiment than did the subjects with a low desire for control. When the nine anagram set options were used as nine-point scales with the higher score indicating a more challenging task, I found that the high desire for control subjects selected a significantly more difficult set of anagrams to work on for their first choice ($M = 6.12$) than the low desire for control subjects ($M = 4.29$). When the three choices were added together, the same pattern emerged, with high desire for control subjects selecting more difficult tasks overall ($M = 19.35$) than the subjects with a low desire for control ($M = 16.23$).

A second experiment also demonstrated this tendency for high desire for control subjects to select more challenging tasks than low desire for control subjects, but also examined how realistically they would adjust their aspiration level on subsequent tasks. Undergraduates received a booklet containing six puzzles. The numbers 1 through 50 were scattered randomly around each puzzle page. Subjects were instructed to connect the numbers sequentially, beginning with 1 and continuing until the 20-second time limit expired. Before turning the page to begin each puzzle, subjects also were asked to estimate how far they would go on the next puzzle. The task was selected because nearly everyone overestimates his or her ability to connect the numbers sequentially on the initial puzzle.

Dependent variables for this experiment were calculated in several ways. First, desire for control was correlated with how far subjects estimated they would get on the first puzzle ($r = .31$), and with the total estimates for the six puzzles ($r = .28$). Thus, as in the earlier study, a high desire for control was associated with higher aspirations. However, I also wanted to know how well subjects would adjust their estimates based on the feedback indicating they had overestimated their abilities. I calculated the absolute difference between the subjects' performance on each trial with their estimate for that test. These numbers were summed to create an overall accuracy index, indicating how well subjects were able to meet their established goal. This index was negatively correlated with DC Scale scores ($r = -.38$). This correlation suggests that although the high desire for control subjects had higher aspirations than the low desire for control subjects, they also were much better at using the feedback from previous trials to estimate how well they would do on subsequent trials.

The higher aspiration level of high desire for control people was also demonstrated in a study in which college students were asked about their grades (Burger, 1991a). I asked freshman and sophomore students during the sixth week of a ten-week fall quarter to estimate what their grade point average would be that quarter and for the overall school year. Desire for Control Scale scores were significantly correlated with both the students' predictions for the quarter ($r = .39$, $p < .001$) and the year ($r = .42$, $p < .001$), with higher estimates associated with higher desire for control. Desire for control also correlated with the number of hours students reported studying in a typical week ($r = .22$, $p < .05$) and how important they felt it was to get good grades ($r = .21$, $p < .05$). Thus, the high desire for control students in this study thought it more important to do well in the area of academic achievement and set their aspiration levels higher than did the low desire for control students.

RESPONSE TO A CHALLENGE

The second step in the model deals with how high desire for control people and low desire for control people deal with unforeseen difficulties or a particularly challenging task. I expected that the more challenging the task, up to a reasonable point, the more high desire for control people would see the task as a threat to their sense of control and an opportunity to demonstrate their personal mastery. The extra effort generated from this perception has the advantage of increasing the likelihood that the task will be achieved. The disadvantage is that these high desire for control people may run the risk of becoming even more dejected if their extra effort fails. Wortman and Brehm (1975) have argued that people typically expend increased effort when controlling a task that is important to them. However, these same people are then more susceptible to negative reactions, most notably depression, if they eventually conclude that the task is not controllable. Because high desire for control people generally believe controlling a challenging achievement task is more important than do low desire for control people, they may be more vulnerable to the consequences of failure at such tasks.

The results from one of my experiments support this reasoning (Burger, 1985). Subjects worked on a proofreading task. They were given 10 minutes to identify and correct all spelling, punctuation, and grammar errors they found on an error-filled manuscript. The task was made particularly challenging for half the subjects, who were told they also needed to keep track of how many times the word *the* appeared and the number of proper nouns they found. At the end of 10 minutes subjects drew a line on the manuscript indicating the last line they had proofread and, in the proper condition, indicated how many times they had seen the word *the* and how many proper nouns they had found.

Interestingly, high desire for control subjects and low desire for control subjects finished about the same number of lines on the proof-reading task in the unchallenging condition. However, the high desire for control subjects did significantly better when the proofreading was made particularly challenging by adding the two extra tasks. I interpret this finding to mean that high desire for control subjects do not necessarily work harder at every task they encounter. Rather, they respond to challenging tasks that either threaten their sense of control or offer an opportunity to demonstrate their mastery.

An interesting twist on this point was made in an unpublished honors project conducted by Mark Wilsmann under my direction at Wake Forest University. Wilsmann adapted a simulated business situation developed by Hegarty and Sims (1978) to look at the effects of desire for control on ethical business behavior. In this simulation, undergraduates had to make a series of business decisions to maximize profits for an imaginary company. At certain points in the simulation subjects were given the opportunity to use illegal kickbacks to increase profits. Wilsmann created two conditions, one that emphasized competition with the other subjects, and one that deemphasized competition. Competition, like other challenges, increases the desire to perform well for high desire for control people.

Overall, there was no correlation between desire for control and the number of times subjects chose to use the illegal kickbacks to increase their profits. However, there was an interaction between desire for control and the competition variable on this measure. High desire for control subjects were just as likely to use the kickbacks in the competitive as in the noncompetitive condition. However, low desire for control subjects gave more kickbacks than high desire for control subjects in the competitive condition and fewer kickbacks than high desire for control subjects in the noncompetitive condition. In other words, the high desire for control subjects did not alter their behavior depending upon the level of competition, whereas the low desire for control subjects were more likely to engage in the unethical behavior when they felt they were in competition than when there was little competition.

Although subjects were merely participating in a simulated business game, the implications from the findings are intriguing. They suggest that high desire for control people do not want to win at any cost. Indeed, we might speculate that succeeding through cheating is not very satisfying for people with a high desire for control. If anything, success through such means might challenge their need to feel as if they are capable of mastering the situation on their own. Subjects with a low desire for control, on the other hand, seemed to respond to the competition by doing whatever was needed to win. Winning through cheating does not appear to have been as much of a concern to them as it was for the highs.

PERSISTENCE

The third step in the model predicts that high desire for control people will persist longer at a difficult task than will people with a low desire for control. Admitting that a task is too challenging or beyond one's ability to master is more difficult for high desire for control people. Admitting failure may be especially difficult when the task appears to be one that can be accomplished with enough effort and ability. Whereas we might expect low desire for control people to quickly decide that they cannot finish a challenging task, such admissions are not easy for people with a high desire for control. The result is that high desire for control people will put in the extra effort and work at the difficult task longer, and thus are more likely to overcome the obstacles and conquer the task than are the low desire for control people. However, these high desire for control people also are more likely to persist at impossible tasks, fail to look for assistance, and generally waste time, effort, and resources when they encounter a task that really is beyond their ability to master.

I tested this step in the model by giving undergraduate subjects a set of problems that appeared solvable, but in fact were not (Burger, 1985). During the first part of the experiment subjects received a booklet containing three cryptoquote puzzles. Cryptoquote puzzles require subjects to figure out the code in a series of letters to form a well-known quote or expression (for example, a B is always an R, an M is always a T, and so on). Subjects were given seven minutes to work on each of the three puzzles in the booklet. A few correct letters were already given on each puzzle, and virtually all subjects completed all three puzzles in the allotted time. Subjects then were given a second booklet containing seven cryptoquote puzzles, one per page. They were told that they had 15 minutes to work on the puzzles. Subjects were told that they could skip ahead to the next puzzle if they had trouble, but they needed to indicate in an appropriate space that they had tried to work on the puzzle but found it too difficult to complete. They also were instructed that they could not return to a puzzle once they had turned past it and that they had to work on the puzzles in order.

In reality, none of the puzzles in the second booklet were solvable. Because no clues were given in the second booklet, subjects found it believable that they suddenly were having difficulty with the task. The dependent variable was how many puzzles the subjects would attempt during the 15 minutes. As expected, the high desire for control subjects worked on significantly fewer puzzles than the low desire for control subjects. In other words, they were less likely than the low desire for control subjects to give up and move on to the next puzzle. This reaction seems particularly likely in this situation because the task appeared to be one that could be accomplished with enough effort. After all, the subjects had done well on the three earlier puzzles, and during debriefing no subjects said it occurred to them that the experimenter might give them unsolvable puzzles. High desire for control people will not waste time on clearly impossible tasks, but they may be less likely to recognize them.

ATTRIBUTIONS

For many years researchers have recognized the role of attributions in achievement behavior (cf. Weiner, 1985b). Generally, higher achievement is associated with giving oneself credit for success and attributing failure to a lack of effort or bad luck. People who make such attributions are more likely to expect success on future tasks and are likely to approach them with higher motivation and more confidence than those who do not make these attributions. My original model proposed that high desire for control people were more likely than low desire for control people to make these kinds of high-achievement attributions and therefore more likely to do well on subsequent tasks. This prediction follows from the notion that high desire for control people are motivated to see themselves as having caused their successes. That is, they want to believe that they can master achievement tasks. On the other hand, these high desire for control people are reluctant to admit that they lack the abilities or skills required to accomplish goals, especially those that other people seem able to reach. Thus, high desire for control people who do poorly at a test or a new game are likely to attribute their failure to something unstable, preferably to something they can do something about in the future, such as a lack of practice.

I tested this by utilizing a guessing-game task developed by Weiner and Kukla (1970). An experimenter explained to undergraduate subjects that he or she would be reading a list of 50 numbers, all either 1 or 0, and the subjects' task would be to guess before each trial which number the experimenter would read next (Burger, 1985). The experimenter explained that the numbers were not arranged randomly, but rather that there were general trends in the order of presentation the subject was to try to figure out. Naturally, in reality the numbers were arranged in a random order. At the end of the task, subjects counted up the number of correct responses and answered some items on a questionnaire. The two key items asked subjects to indicate how many of the correct guesses were the result of skill rather than luck, and how many correct guesses they would make if they did the task again with a different set of numbers.

Because performance on the guessing game was, in fact, chance determined, subjects naturally averaged about 25 correct guesses, with some doing better and some doing worse. Subjects were trichotomized into success, average, and failure categories depending upon their correct number of guesses. As shown in Table 5-2, high desire for control subjects were more likely than low desire for control subjects to think that their correct guesses had been the result of their skill at determining the general patterns in the list of numbers. In addition, this belief appeared to translate into significantly more confidence that they would do better on a second list than shown by the subjects with a low desire for control.

Thus, the findings suggest that high desire for control people are more likely than low desire for control people to make the kinds of attributions that are likely to lead to higher motivation (and consequently higher success) on subsequent tasks. However, two subsequent experiments have challenged part of this conclusion (Burger, 1987c). First, students enrolled in an undergraduate social psychology course completed two questionnaires on the day tests were returned for the second of three course examinations. Before receiving the test, students indicated what grade they would be satisfied with. After examining their tests, subjects were asked to indicate in open-ended and Likert-scale items the reasons for their performance on the test.

The students had taken the DC Scale earlier as part of what they believed to be unrelated data collection. Students were divided into those who had performed as well as they had wanted or better (success) and those who had not reached the grade that they said they would have

TABLE 5-2. Reactions to Performance on Number-Guessing Task

	Failure		Average		Success	
	High desire for control	Low desire for control	High desire for control	Low desire for control	High desire for control	Low desire for control
Correct guesses attributed to skill	5.27	4.62	8.57	7.00	20.14	12.20
Correct guesses for another task	26.67	25.50	33.71	27.57	36.42	34.40

Note: From Burger (1985); copyright © 1985 by the American Psychological Association; reprinted by permission of the publisher

been satisfied with (failure). The open-ended attributions were coded for the extent to which they were internal versus external, that is, if the subjects attributed their performance to something about themselves (for example, effort) or some external source (for example, the instructor). In addition, the attributions were coded as either stable (for example, ability) or unstable (for example, luck). Finally, I looked at how well subjects did on the next test, given about three weeks later.

The students gave attributions for their performances on the test consistent with the model. High desire for control students tended to make internal and stable attributions for their successes, but gave external and unstable attributions when they believed that they had not done well. Thus, a good grade likely was interpreted as the result of one's intelligence, but a poor grade was blamed on having an unusually bad week. In contrast, the attributions of the students with a low desire for control did not change as a function of how well they thought they had done on the test.

However, when I looked at how the students did on the next test, two interesting and unpredicted findings emerged. First, the students who did the best on the next test were the high desire for control students who had not done well on the earlier test. In contrast, the low desire for control students who had done well on the initial test performed better on the next test than the low desire for control students who thought they had done poorly. Second, contrary to the model, analyses of covariance revealed that the attributions subjects made for their performances on the previous test had no apparent effect whatsoever on how well they did on the next test.

Before interpreting these findings, I conducted a similar experiment in the more controlled laboratory environment (Burger, 1987c). Undergraduates worked on digit-symbol tests similar to those used in the Wechsler Adult Intelligence Scales. The test presents a code in which symbols are paired with the numbers 1 through 9. Subjects are required to draw the symbol that is associated with each of 100 randomly presented numbers. The experimenter rigged the outcome the first time subjects took the test so that everyone believed he or she had received a score of 55. Subjects then were given feedback indicating that a score of 55 placed them either in the 85th percentile (success) or 15th percentile (failure) for college students. Subjects then were asked to list the reasons for their performance and were given a second digit-symbol test. This time all subjects were given 90 seconds to complete the test. A control group took the second test only.

Just as in the earlier study, high desire for control subjects gave more internal attributions when they thought that they had done well than when they had failed. And once again, subjects with a low desire for control did not change their attributions as a result of their performance. However, the same two unpredicted findings uncovered in the earlier experiment also emerged. That is, as shown in Table 5-3, high desire for control subjects did better on the second test when they thought they had done poorly on the first one than when they thought they had done well. And again, the analyses of covariance indicated that the attributions subjects made for their initial performances had little if any impact on their performances on the next test.

What can we say about the original model, given this consistent evidence contradicting it? One part of the model seems intact. High desire for control people do appear to make attributions in a manner that satisfies their need to feel that they are able to master challenging tasks. However, whether these attributions then lead to changes in subsequent performances is questionable. Instead, what the two Burger (1987c) studies suggest is that high desire for control subjects respond to unsuccessful experiences with increased effort, a type of reactance effect (see Chapter 4). Although not initially anticipated, these findings make sense in terms of the descriptions of high desire for control people and low desire for control people. Doing a task poorly that a person believes he or she should be able to do well is more threatening to a high desire for control person than to a person with a low desire for control. High desire for control students who do poorly on a midterm exam become highly motivated to demonstrate that they can do well on the final exam. Low desire for control students who fail the same midterm exam are more likely to accept the low grade, perhaps saying to themselves that the subject matter is just too difficult, or that they simply lack the ability to do any better. Finally, low desire for control subjects in the two studies did better on the second task when they felt that they

TABLE 5-3. Performance on Subsequent Tasks
after Success and Failure Experiences

	Success		Failure		Control	
	High desire for control	Low desire for control	High desire for control	Low desire for control	High desire for control	Low desire for control
Grade on next course exam	49.40	50.10	53.30	48.92	—	—
Score on next digit symbol test	62.69	70.23	69.64	64.79	60.57	64.36

Note: From Burger (1987c)

had done well on the first task. This improvement may simply reflect the effects of positive reinforcement.

In summary, most of the original model I developed to explain the relationship between desire for control and achievement behavior has been supported with a series of experiments. Compared to people with a low desire for control, high desire for control people were found to have higher aspiration levels, to adjust their aspirations more realistically following feedback, to respond with more effort to challenging tasks, and to persist longer at difficult tasks. Although the high desire for control subjects and the low desire for control subjects in these studies tended to make attributions for their performances in the expected pattern, it is not clear that these attributions play a role in how much they try or how well they do on subsequent tasks. Nonetheless, none of the research reviewed thus far answers the question of who actually achieves more, high desire for control people or low desire for control people. I turn to that question next.

WHO ACHIEVES MORE?

The most reasonable answer to this question would seem to be that under certain conditions high desire for control people will do better, but under other conditions we can expect people with a low desire for control to achieve more. For example, when the task is a challenging one calling for a little persistence, a person with a high desire for control is likely to do better. However, if a particular facet of a task is in reality insurmountable, then the low desire for control person is more likely than the high desire for control person to acknowledge this limitation and put his or her efforts into more achievable endeavors.

But the question remains: In the real world, who is likely to do better? In the types of achievement situations typically encountered in our society, such as in academic settings or on the job, would the high desire for control or the low desire for control approach tend to be more productive? The only solid data to date addressing this question come from the study in which students were asked to estimate their grades for the upcoming quarter and year (Burger, 1991a). These students also gave me permission to examine their academic records two years from the time of the testing. Thus, I could see how well desire for control scores predicted their academic performance.

I divided subjects into high desire for control and low desire for control halves and compared the two groups for average grade point average for the first year, the second year, and the total of the two years following the administration of the DC Scale. As shown in Table 5-4, the subjects with a high desire for control performed better academically on each of these measures. Another way of looking at the relationship between desire for control and grades is to look at the number of students reaching a 3.00 grade point average (on a four-point scale) for the two-year period. This analysis found that whereas 55% of the high desire for control subjects reached this level of academic achievement, only 11.1% of the low desire for control subjects did ($p < .01$).

Given the large number of factors that can affect a student's grades, the findings from the study suggest a strong link between desire for control and academic achievement. Naturally, in this study there is no way to rule out the possibility that the students' earlier experiences with academic success may have contributed to their higher desire for control. Nonetheless, having a high desire for control does not appear to interfere with a college student's ability to do well academically, and quite probably aids him or her in this quest.

INTRINSIC MOTIVATION

For the past few decades, many researchers have found it useful to dichotomize motivation for achievement-oriented tasks into intrinsic and extrinsic motivation. The original formulations of this approach described intrinsically motivated behavior as that we engage in to satisfy personal needs, such as demonstrating personal mastery and competence or satisfying curiosity (Deci, 1975; Lepper & Greene, 1978). In contrast, we engage in extrinsically motivated behavior to receive external rewards, such as money or praise. Thus, the girl who plays the piano because she enjoys the experience is intrinsically motivated, but the boy who plays the piano because his parents pay him to practice is extrinsically motivated.

Early work in this area demonstrated that introducing extrinsic rewards typically lowers a person's intrinsic interest in the activity. That is, if we pay people to do something they already enjoy, they will be less likely to engage in that behavior when not paid. This effect has been

TABLE 5-4. Mean Grade Point Averages

	High desire for control	Low desire for control	p
First-year grades	2.91	2.68	.05
Second-year grades	2.99	2.73	.001
Two-year total grades	2.94	2.71	.001

Note: From Burger (1991a)

demonstrated in a number of experiments. Typically, subjects are either paid or not paid to engage in an interesting activity, such as working on puzzles. Then the experimenter leaves the room for a few minutes, allowing the subject the opportunity to continue the task or not. The experimenter often watches through a one-way window and records the amount of time spent on the target activity. Numerous experiments using this basic procedure have demonstrated that subjects originally paid to engage in the activity are less likely to continue on the task when the experimenter leaves the room than are those who were not paid. The paid subjects are said to have had their intrinsic interest in the activity undermined by the introduction of the extrinsic reward.

Deci (1975) originally described intrinsic motivation in terms similar to a need for control. Later, as described in Chapter 1, he changed his position slightly to emphasize that it was not control *per se* that people were after, but rather a sense of self-determination (Deci, 1980; Deci & Ryan, 1985a). Desire for control appears to be very similar to Deci's notion of self-determination. Thus, if we apply individual differences in desire for control to the question of intrinsic and extrinsic motivation, we would expect that people with a high desire for control would more often and more intensely express intrinsic motivation than someone with a low desire for control. High desire for control people should have a stronger need to demonstrate to themselves that they are masterful manipulators of their environment. Consequently, high desire for control people may be more likely than low desire for control people to try brain teasers and crossword puzzles because of the sense of mastery that comes from arriving at solutions to these challenges. Evidence to support this expectation comes from two sources. First, we can look at correlations between desire for control and relevant individual difference measures. Second, we can use laboratory experiments to examine how high desire for control people and low desire for control people react to the introduction of extrinsic rewards for intrinsically interesting tasks.

CORRELATIONS WITH INDIVIDUAL DIFFERENCE MEASURES

If high desire for control people generally are more interested in establishing a sense of mastery and competence in achievement situations than low desire for control people, then we would expect desire for control scores to correlate with some of the subscales on the Work and Family Orientation (WOFO) Questionnaire (Spence & Helmreich, 1983). The WOFO was designed to measure three components of achievement motivation. The Work subscale measures the desire to work hard and to do a good job. People scoring high on the Mastery subscale have a preference for difficult, challenging tasks. More important, this subscale also was designed to measure the extent to which people generally work to feel masterful and meet internal standards of excellence. In other words, high scorers are more likely than low scorers to be intrinsically motivated to overcome a challenging task. Finally, the Competition subscale measures how much the test taker enjoys competition and winning in achievement situations.

I administered the DC Scale and the WOFO to 98 undergraduates in an unpublished study. As shown in Table 5-5, desire for control was significantly related to all three of the subscales. I found a particularly strong correlation between desire for control and the Mastery score. This finding is consistent with the notion that the need for self-determination, as reflected in one's desire for control score, is an important factor underlying intrinsically motivated behavior.

Another relevant set of personality scales was developed by Deci and Ryan (1985b). As part of their research on self-determination and intrinsic motivation, Deci and Ryan constructed the General Causality Orientation Scale. The scale generates three subscale scores on autonomy orientation, control orientation, and impersonal orientation. People scoring high on autonomy orientation tend to seek out opportunities to express their self-determination and personal choice. They are likely to demonstrate a high level of intrinsic motivation. Those scoring high on control orientation tend to do things because they think they are supposed to. They are more likely than most people to be motivated by extrinsic pressures, such as a boss's scorn or a deadline. Finally, high scorers on impersonal orientation do not believe they are able to control outcomes. They may see themselves as unable to master situations.

I administered the DC Scale and the General Causality Orientation Scale to a group of undergraduates. As shown in Table 5-6, two small but significant correlations were found in this unpublished study. A high desire for control was associated with a tendency to seek out opportunities to demonstrate one's mastery over the environment, and negatively correlated with feelings that one was incapable of mastering situations.

TABLE 5-5. Correlations between DC Scale
and WOFO Subscale Scores

Subscale	Males	Females	Total sample
Work	.17	.29*	.23*
Mastery	.51**	.49*	.51**
Competition	.42**	.23	.32**

Note: Sample = 42 males and 56 female undergraduates; * $p < .05$; ** $p < .01$

TABLE 5-6. Correlations between DC Scale
and General Causality Orientation Scale

Scale	r with DC Scale	p
Autonomy orientation	.18	.025
Control orientation	.04	ns
Impersonal orientation	−.28	.001

Note: Sample = 120 male and female undergraduates

Similar correlations were reported recently by Thompson (1990). In a sample of 67 undergraduates, he found correlations of .36, .18, and −.37 between desire for control and the autonomy, control, and impersonal orientation scales, respectively.

Taken together, the pattern of correlations between the DC Scale and the WOFO and General Causality Orientation scales is consistent with the notion that high desire for control people are generally more likely than low desire for control people to engage in an achievement task in order to satisfy their need to feel competent and masterful. But I would argue that not only are high desire for control people more attracted to tasks that can satisfy these needs, they are more likely than low desire for control people to react to threats to their sense of self-determination. That is, high desire for control people should not be very interested in a task when they perceive that their participation is controlled by extrinsic rewards. Thus, as examined in the next section, I would expect high desire for control people to be more vulnerable than low desire for control people to an undermining of their intrinsic motivation with extrinsic reinforcers.

REACTION TO EXTRINSIC REWARDS

Researchers have identified a number of variables that interfere with or undermine experimental subjects' level of intrinsic motivation. The most commonly demonstrated variable remains the introduction of extrinsic rewards, especially when the rewards are expected and contingent on performance. Other variables that have been found to undermine intrinsic motivation include surveillance, threats, deadlines, and positive feedback (Deci & Ryan, 1987). In each case, the salient extrinsic source of motivation is said to lead to the perception that the behavior is no longer self-determined. Because high desire for control people have a stronger need for self-determination, I expected them to have a stronger reaction to this manipulation than people with a low desire for control.

This prediction has been tested in two experiments using the introduction-of-rewards procedure. Undergraduates in the first of these experiments were either paid or not paid to play Labyrinth, a marble-maze game (Burger, 1980). The experimenter then left subjects alone in the experimental room while he or she supposedly went to photocopy some more questionnaires. Subjects were told they could play with the Labyrinth game, read some magazines that were lying on a nearby table, or anything else they wanted while the experimenter was gone. The experimenter then observed subjects for eight minutes through a one-way window to time how much they played with the game in the absence of reward. The subjects also completed several scale items indicating their amount of interest in playing the Labyrinth game once the experimenter returned with the questionnaires.

No differences were found in terms of how long subjects actually played with the game. However, I found the pattern shown in Table 5-7 when the questionnaire items were summed for an overall self-report motivation score. As seen in the table, whether they were paid did not appear to affect the interest in the game of the subjects with a low desire for control. However, as anticipated, high desire for control subjects reported significantly less interest in the game when they had been paid to play it earlier than when no payment was given.

Recently, Thompson (1990) utilized a similar procedure to evaluate the effects of extrinsic rewards on intrinsic motivation for high desire for control people and people with a low desire for control. Subjects in this experiment were either paid or not paid to engage in a series of brainstorming puzzles in which they tried to think of uses for common objects. The major dependent variable was how many seconds subjects would work on an extra set of brainstorming puzzles during the six minutes when the experimenter left the room. Consistent with my earlier finding, high desire for control subjects were significantly less interested in the task when they had been paid than when they had received no pay. However, Thompson also found a complete crossover interaction with low desire for control subjects showing a strong interest in the brainstorming puzzles when paid, but relatively little interest when not paid. This latter finding is curious, and may suggest that low desire for control people are more comfortable with tasks they perceive to be extrinsically

TABLE 5-7. Self-Report Motivation Scores

	High desire for control	Low desire for control
Payment condition	11.33	8.27
No-Payment condition	8.67	7.76

Note: Lower scores indicate a higher level of interest in the game; from Burger (1980)

oriented than those they believe to be self-determined. Nonetheless, the high desire for control subjects in both experiments showed the preference for self-determined activities and resistance to controlled behavior I anticipated.

Should we conclude from these findings that high desire for control people are rarely satisfied with their extrinsically rewarded jobs and constantly fly from one interest to another as they become aware of the extrinsic reasons for doing their work? Fortunately, the answer is probably no. It is possible to retain a sense of self-determination even in situations with extrinsic reinforcers. After all, the students with a high desire for control in the earlier study did better in classes which reward performance with grades. However, it probably also is the case that high desire for control people will be less content with a job that does not give them a large sense of self-determination. Similarly, high desire for control people are probably more likely than people with a low desire for control to react negatively to the introduction of such controlling sources as surveillance and deadlines. Most likely, high desire for control people and low desire for control people select jobs that best meet their personal needs.

SUMMARY

The research reviewed in this chapter clearly illustrates that desire for control is tied to achievement motivation and achievement behaviors in many ways. High desire for control people approach achievement tasks differently than people with a low desire for control. They set higher standards for themselves and are more motivated to overcome challenging tasks in an effort to demonstrate their personal mastery. High desire for control people also have a different style of working on a task than low desire for control people. They seem to be better able to adjust their goals realistically, and they respond to challenges with more effort and greater persistence. Once the task is completed, high desire for control people attribute successes and failures to different causes than do low desire for control people. Moreover, they seem to respond to perceived failure by working all the harder on the next task. Although there are tasks that meet the needs and work habits of both high desire for control people and low desire for control people, it may be the case that in the typical work setting high desire for control people achieve more.

High desire for control people also are probably more likely than low desire for control people to engage in a task for intrinsically motivated reasons. They are more likely than low desire for control people to work at a puzzle or game because of the satisfaction that comes with demonstrating their competence and ability to master the challenge. Consequently, high desire for control people are more susceptible to an undermining of their intrinsic motivation with the introduction of extrinsic rewards.

CHAPTER 6

ATTRIBUTIONS AND INFORMATION PROCESSING

Attribution theory has been called "the dominant theoretical perspective" in social psychology (Aron & Aron, 1986). For more than a quarter of a decade now, the study of how people go about explaining the causes of their own and other people's behavior has been a cornerstone of social psychology research. Work on attributions began as an extension of research on person perception, but the applications of some of the findings soon became apparent to psychologists working in other areas. Consequently, understanding the attributions people make for themselves and the behavior of others has proven quite useful in understanding such diverse topics as depression, educational achievement, and relationships.

The research reported in this chapter was designed to examine the relationship between desire for control and the use of causal attributions. More specifically, three questions are addressed. First, do high desire for control people and low desire for control people differ in their likelihood of engaging in attributional activity? Second, are there consistently different patterns in the types of attributions people with a high desire for control and people with a low desire for control use to explain events? Third, is there a relationship between desire for control and the tendency to succumb to attributional errors? That is, are high desire for control people or low desire for control people more prone to distorting their attributions in a way that satisfies their need to feel in control over the events in their lives? As will be seen, the relevant research on these questions to date provides some fairly clear answers.

101

ATTRIBUTIONAL ACTIVITY

Much of the early work on attributional processes operated on the assumption that people engaged in nearly constant attributional activity. Researchers assumed that each of us is continually engaged in rather spontaneous searches for the causes to each and every behavior we come into contact with. However, these researchers soon recognized that their subjects did not always react to their experimental situations with active attributional activity. In fact, other investigators and I found that we often had to prompt our subjects with the correctly phrased questions before they provided some of these spontaneous attributions. Consequently, some researchers began to examine another question—the conditions under which people do and do not engage in efforts to understand the causes of behavior (cf. Weiner, 1985a).

Many of the circumstances that lead to an attributional search have been identified in this work, such as when the behavior is unexpected. However, the question remains as to *why* people ask themselves "Why?" Extensive attributional activity requires more effort than most of us typically are willing to expend. In fact, recent theorizing about attributional processes suggests that we operate more in a cognitive miser mode, using heuristics and shortcuts to give us a sense of understanding rather than collecting and examining all of the information needed to come up with accurate accounts for why a certain behavior occurred (Gilbert, 1989).

However, common sense tells us that at least on some occasions we do engage in elaborate searches for the causes of behavior. Why? One explanation is that attributions allow us to obtain or maintain a sense of control (Kelley, 1971; Wortman, 1976). Clearly, if we are to control the important events in our lives, it is necessary that we understand why those events occurred. How can I maintain a sense of control if I have no idea why my business competitor, my spouse, my students, my boss, or my friends act the way they do? Maintaining a sense of control is probably impossible unless we feel we have at least some understanding of why important events happen.

One hypothesis derived from this line of reasoning is that the stronger a person's need to feel in control of an event, the more he or she will engage in attributional activity to better understand why the event happened. Several investigations have found support for this hypothesis by manipulating the extent to which people are motivated to control experimental situations (Liu & Steele, 1986; Pittman & Pittman, 1980; Swann, Stephenson, & Pittman, 1981). Generally these researchers find that depriving subjects of a sense of control, and hence increasing their need to regain a sense of control, leads to greater attributional activity.

We can step logically from the reasoning behind these investigations to suggest that high desire for control people typically engage in more attributional activity than people with a low desire for control. High desire for control people generally are more motivated to feel as if they are in control of the events in their environment. Their sense of control is challenged when they are unable to understand immediately the causes of important, unexpected, or otherwise curious events. In addition, high desire for control people are more likely than low desire for control people to be engaged in a type of vigilant information processing about the events they encounter. Whereas low desire for control people are more likely to ignore the actions of others until it becomes necessary, high desire for control people are likely to engage in a constant scanning of their worlds to see if there is some important information out there that may threaten their sense of control.

Support for this hypothesis comes from two sources. First, I examine studies looking at correlations between desire for control scores and measures of individual differences in cognitive and attributional activity. Second, I look at how experimental subjects have reacted to situational manipulations designed to stimulate and assess the extent to which they engage in the processing of attributional information.

CORRELATIONS WITH INDIVIDUAL DIFFERENCE MEASURES

If high desire for control people are more likely than low desire for control people to engage in attributional activity, then scores on the DC Scale should correlate positively with measures of general cognitive activity. One relevant scale was developed by Cacioppo, Petty, and Kao (1984) to measure individual differences in "an individual's tendency to engage in and enjoy effortful cognitive endeavors." The Need for Cognition Scale was not designed to assess intelligence, but rather the extent to which people prefer to deliberate, contemplate, and generally think about ideas and various options and opinions. Thus, someone with a high need for cognition would prefer games like chess rather than bingo and movies that make them think rather than those that are merely entertaining. Attitude change researchers have found the scale differentiates those who typically accept persuasive messages and those who think about and elaborate on the arguments (Cacioppo, Petty, Kao, & Rodriguez, 1986).

I am aware of seven studies that have examined the relationship between the DC Scale and the Need for Cognition Scale, including one unpublished study of my own. As shown in Table 6-1, the correlations reported in these studies reveal a remarkably consistent pattern. Desire

TABLE 6-1. Correlations between DC Scale and Need for Cognition Scale

Sample size	r	Source
125	.47	Chaikin (personal communication, October 18, 1988)
106	.46	Burger (unpublished)
202	.51	Thompson (1990)
194	.36	Thompson (1990)
123	.51	Maheswaran (cited in Thompson, 1990)
153	.47	Axsom (cited in Thompson, 1990)
334	.45	Thompson (personal communication, December 9, 1990)

for control appears to be positively correlated with the need for cognition. The consistency of the findings and the size of the samples indicates that the relationship is a strong and reliable one.

Another relevant individual difference measure was developed by Fletcher, Danilovics, Fernandez, Peterson, and Reeder (1986). These researchers created the Attributional Complexity Scale to assess the extent to which people typically engage in complex attributional activity and understand the complexity of causes involved in explaining human behavior. People scoring high on the scale tend to be curious about the causes of behavior, consider many variables before making attributions, and shun simple answers when trying to understand their own and other people's actions. Fletcher *et al.* report a correlation of .36 between their scale and the Need for Cognition Scale.

I administered the Attributional Complexity Scale to the 106 undergraduates in the unpublished study referred to in Table 6-1. As predicted, desire for control correlated significantly with attributional complexity, $r = .27$. I also found a positive correlation between need for cognition and attributional complexity, $r = .32$. Recently, Thompson (1990) reported finding an even stronger correlation between desire for control and attributional complexity in two separate samples. He uncovered a correlation between the two scales of .44 ($p < .001$) with a sample of 61 undergraduates and a correlation of .50 ($p < .001$) with a second sample of 64 undergraduates.

Taken together, the pattern of correlations indicates that high desire for control people generally are more likely than low desire for control people to engage in an extensive search for explanations for behavior and events. Naturally, although these correlations are consistent with the predictions, like all correlational data they provide only weak support for the hypothesis. However, the conclusions to be drawn from these studies are bolstered by the findings from a series of laboratory experiments examining the attributional activity of high desire for control subjects and low desire for control subjects when presented with various events for which they might want to search for explanations.

ATTRIBUTIONAL ACTIVITY IN LABORATORY EXPERIMENTS

Clues about why other people do the things they do are sometimes so subtle that they are likely to be missed by all but those keenly interested in understanding the reasons behind the behavior. If high desire for control people typically engage in more attributional activity than low desire for control people, then they should be more likely to perceive and utilize this attributionally relevant information. I tested this prediction in a laboratory experiment (Burger & Hemans, 1988). We employed the procedures used earlier by Pittman and Pittman (1980), in which subjects read an essay about the advantages of developing nuclear energy. The author was supposedly a nuclear engineer who had worked in the area for 25 years. The key independent variable was the presence of information at the beginning of the material that would help subjects better understand the reasons why the author took the position he did. Half of the subjects read that the author was paid $2,500 to write an article from which the essay was taken, half were told the essay came from the writer's private journal and was not originally intended for publication. The question was whether subjects would use this information in later answering questions about how the author really feels about the issue, or if they would instead rely on a cognitively efficient heuristic that says what people do usually reflects what they believe.

Subjects answered several questionnaire items after reading the author information and essay, including items asking them to rate the extent to which they thought the essay was written because of the characteristics and opinions of the author or because of some external influences. As expected, high desire for control subjects and low desire for control subjects differed in the extent to which they used the earlier information in making these attributions. High desire for control subjects tended to make external attributions for the writer's behavior when they had been informed that the writer was paid for his essay. On the other hand, when high desire for control subjects read that the essay was taken from a private journal, they tended to make internal attributions. In contrast, attributions for the author's behavior by low desire for control subjects did not change as a function of which information they received. These subjects apparently failed to use the information about the money or the private journal when explaining why the author had written the essay. Thus, the high desire for control subjects were the ones who attended to and used the attributionally relevant information.

A second experiment was concerned with whether high desire for control people and low desire for control people differ in the extent to which they ask questions that help them make attributions for other people's behavior (Burger & Hemans, 1988). Some information is more relevant for understanding the causes of behavior than others. For example, if I meet a man who is rude to me, knowing whether this person also is rude to other people or on other occasions will help me make an accurate attribution for his behavior. We hypothesized that high desire for control people are more likely than low desire for control people to ask themselves these kinds of questions.

To test this hypothesis, we adopted a procedure previously employed by Wong and Weiner (1981). Undergraduates read about four hypothetical situations in which they were to imagine themselves. Two of the scenarios dealt with receiving a midterm examination, one with the grade of A and the other with an F. The other two situations concerned meeting someone at a social gathering, one in which the new acquaintance says something nice about the subject and one in which unkind things are said. Subjects responded to each hypothetical situation by answering the open-ended question, "What questions, if any, would you ask yourself in this situation?" The instructions emphasized that subjects were free to write no questions if that is how they would respond to the situation.

We coded each question as to whether it would help the subject obtain attributionally relevant information. That is, using the coding procedures developed by Wong and Weiner (1981), we identified questions whose answers would be useful in understanding why the behavior had occurred. For example, asking how many As or Fs the teacher typically hands out was coded as an attributionally relevant question because knowing the answer to this question would be helpful in making an attribution for why the grade was received. On the other hand, asking if there was going to be a make-up test would not help the subject better understand his or her performance, and was not coded as an attributionally relevant question.

As expected, high desire for control subjects asked significantly more attributionally relevant questions than subjects with a low desire for control. Although subjects asked more of these questions in the negative-outcome conditions than in the positive-outcome conditions, as found in earlier research, this did not interact with the desire for control variable. In other words, regardless of the hypothetical situation, high desire for control subjects were more likely to seek out information that would help them understand why they had done well or poorly on the test, or why the new acquaintance had said nice or unkind things about them.

Wendy Elrick (personal communications, 1989) attempted to replicate this study using a sample of Australian students at the University of Wollongong. As in our research, she found that high desire for control subjects asked more attributionally relevant questions than low desire for control subjects. However, she also uncovered a significant interaction indicating that the effect was largely limited to negative events. That is, in the Australian sample, high desire for control subjects and low desire for control subjects did not differ in the amount of attributionally relevant information they sought for outcomes with positive conditions, but high desire for control subjects asked more of these questions than low desire for control subjects when dealing with situations with negative outcomes. This finding is not completely surprising, because several earlier studies have found that unexpected and unsuccessful situations are the ones that are most likely to lead to an attributional search (Weiner, 1985a). It may have been that the positive outcomes failed to reach a critical threshold for attributional searching for the subjects in this study. Nonetheless, taken together, the studies support the prediction that high desire for control people are more likely than low desire for control people to seek out attributionally relevant information, at least in some circumstances.

Finally, we looked at the number of attributions people make for their performances (Burger & Hemans, 1988). Although researchers often measure attributions as if people generate one and only one answer when trying to explain behavior, a little reflection on our own experiences should tell us otherwise. For almost any incident worthy of an extensive attributional search, many variables have come together, sometimes in complex ways, to cause the behavior. For example, doing poorly on a test may be the result of not having studied enough. But one could also say that he or she did not study enough because the instructor did not indicate that much studying was necessary, because one was ill, because one's roommates were throwing a party, because of personal problems, because of two other tests that week, and so on. We reasoned that high desire for control people, who engage in more extensive attributional processing, would be less satisfied than low desire for control people with simple answers to their attributional questions. Rather, these high desire for control people are more likely to come up with a large number of sometimes complex explanations for the behaviors they are trying to understand.

We tested this prediction by administering a "general information and cognitive abilities" test to groups of undergraduate students. The test consisted of 50 items, some relatively easy and some rather difficult, requiring knowledge and simple math calculations (for example, "The number of planets in our solar system, + 12 squared + the number of hours in a week"). After working on the problems for 15 minutes, subjects handed in their tests and completed some unrelated personality inventories. While the personality inventories were being taken, the experimenter pretended to score the test. He randomly scored half the tests indicating that the subject had fallen into the 85th percentile for college students, and half indicating a score in the 15th percentile. After the corrected tests were passed back, subjects completed a questionnaire asking them to indicate, among other things, the reasons for their performance on the test. As predicted, high desire for control subjects gave significantly more attributions for their test performance than did subjects with a low desire for control. This was the case regardless of whether they had received feedback indicating a good or a poor performance.

Taken together, the studies reviewed in this section provide fairly consistent evidence that high desire for control people are more likely to engage in attributional activity than are low desire for control people. High desire for control people appear more likely to attend to attributionally relevant information, to ask questions that will help them make attributions for their own and other people's behavior, and to generate more attributions. No doubt there are situations in which both high desire for control people and low desire for control people engage in nearly identical amounts of attributional activity. Extremely important events, such as an unexpected dissolution of a romantic relationship, probably lead all of us to a very extensive search for answers. And mundane life experiences probably go unanalyzed even by those with the highest need for control. However, for all of the events that fall in between these extremes, it seems the higher a person's desire for control, the more likely he or she will seek out relevant information and make attributions to better understand why the behavior occurred.

CHARACTERISTIC ATTRIBUTION PATTERNS

High desire for control people and low desire for control people not only differ in their amount of attributional activity, research indicates that they also typically rely on different kinds of attributions to explain the events they encounter. Evidence for this conclusion comes from several investigations, some of which have been covered elsewhere. For example, in Chapter 5 I described an experiment in which subjects guessed which number, either 0 or 1, an experimenter would read next from a list of 50 numbers (Burger, 1985). High desire for control subjects were more likely than lows to attribute their correct guesses to skill than to luck. Because they believed their success was the result of an ability to detect patterns in the list rather than luck, these high desire for control subjects also predicted they would do better on a subsequent new list of numbers than did the low desire for control subjects.

A similar finding was uncovered in an experiment by Zenker and Berman (1982). These researchers asked subjects to guess before each of 30 trials which of two letters would be flashed on a screen. The investigators manipulated the feedback after each trial to inform each subject that he or she had guessed correctly on 15 of the 30 trials. Subjects then were asked about their performance and rated on separate scales the extent to which they thought their performance was the result of luck, ability, effort, and task difficulty.

Consistent with expectations, desire for control scores correlated positively with the extent to which subjects attributed their performance ability ($r = .30$) and effort ($r = .41$), and negatively with the extent to which they explained their performance as the result of luck ($r = -.51$). The high desire for control subjects tended to attribute their performance to their own ability at such tasks or to the amount of effort they put into the task. However, these high desire for control subjects were not at all likely to say that their performance was the result of luck.

Similar patterns have been found in research that looks at attributions for specific tasks and for performance on a midterm examination (Burger, 1987c) and at correlations between desire for control and measures of attributional style (Burger, 1985). In short, high desire for control people tend to interpret the causes of their behavior in a way that helps them maintain the perception that they are able to control this event and are likely to control similar events in the future. As long as they believe the outcome of the next tennis match or math test is up to their own ability and effort and not external forces, high desire for control people approach those events with the necessary sense of personal control.

Finally, it is interesting to note that desire for control scores also correlated with the extent to which subjects in the Zenker and Berman (1982) letter-guessing experiment felt they had control over the outcome of the task ($r = .40$). In truth, subjects had no control over how well they would do on this experimenter-controlled task. As such, attributions to ability or effort indicate an illusion of control on the part of the high desire for control subjects. As seen in the next section, this tendency to see themselves as having more control over events than they really do may be characteristic of people with a high desire for control.

ATTRIBUTIONAL ERRORS AND ACCURACY

The models for generating and testing hypotheses about the sources of causality outlined by early attribution theorists seemed to suggest that, given enough information, people are capable of arriving at a fairly accurate picture of why they and other people do the things they do. However, research testing some of these models soon recognized that people presented with sufficient information to make accurate attributions nonetheless often arrive at the wrong answer. Moreover, researchers identified several systematic errors in the way we process attributionally relevant information. For example, under certain conditions we tend to underestimate the role of the situation in explaining other people's actions, give ourselves more credit than we deserve for a group project, believe that most people share our opinions and characteristics, and see ourselves as less vulnerable to traumatic experiences than others. The many ways in which we arrive at these and other inaccurate or distorted notions are generally known as attributional *errors* or *biases*.

The mechanisms underlying these errors in our attributional processing remain the source of research and debate (Funder, 1987). However, there are reasons to suspect that sometimes how accurately a person is able to determine the causes of behavior may be a function of the person's level of desire for control. In particular, high desire for control people should be motivated to make attributions that satisfy their need to see themselves in control of the events in their lives. Although this tendency may at times lead them to make relatively accurate attributions for their behavior, it also may cause them to distort the real reasons for their own or someone else's actions. I have examined how desire for control affects attributional errors in three general areas: the illusion of control, attributions for others' control, and attributions about oneself relative to others.

THE ILLUSION OF CONTROL

As described in more detail in Chapter 9, research using a variety of procedures demonstrates that under certain circumstances people typically believe they have more control over events than objectively justified. The clearest example of this illusion of control is found when subjects believe they have some control over events that should be obviously determined by chance, such as lotteries and coin tosses (Langer, 1975). I reasoned that if high desire for control people are more motivated than low desire for control people to see themselves in control of events, then they should be more susceptible to the illusion of control.

Before looking at attributions for events determined by chance we can ask if high desire for control people generally believe they have more control over events than people with a low desire for control, even when this perception is incorrect. I examined this question in an unpublished study using an experimental procedure developed by Alloy and Abramson (1979). Although the procedure is elaborate, essentially subjects make responses on a series of trials that may or may not lead to an increased likelihood that a light will be turned on for that trial. Following a large number of trials, subjects estimate the extent to which they were able to alter the likelihood that the light would go on or not by making or not making a response on a given trial. The interesting finding from the Alloy and Abramson studies is that mildly depressed subjects were more accurate in gauging their ability to control the onset of the light than were nondepressed subjects.

I modified the Alloy and Abramson procedure to examine the effect of desire for control on subjects' assessments of their level of control over the onset of the light. Forty-three male and female undergraduates served as subjects. Using the lengthy description of the procedure provided by Alloy and Abramson (1979), I explained to subjects that they would have the opportunity to respond or not respond on each of 40 trials. Each trial began with the onset of a yellow light. At this time subjects had three seconds to either make a response (placing a poker chip on the apparatus in front of them) or not. A green light either would or would not come on after three seconds.

Subjects were randomly assigned to one of two contingency schedules. In the 75–50 condition, the light came on 75% of the time when subjects made a response, but only half of the time if they made no response. Thus, if subjects had perceived these contingencies correctly, they would have seen that they had 25% control above pure chance of whether the light would come on for any given trial. In the 75–0 condition, the light came on 75% of the time after a response, but never came on when no response was made. Subjects who accurately perceived these contingencies would have seen that they had significantly more control over the onset of the light than did subjects in the other condition.

After the 40 trials, subjects were shown a 101-point continuum with labels ranging from no control at 0 to complete control at 100. They were asked to place an X to indicate how much control they thought they had over whether or not the light would come on. As shown in Table 6-2, two significant main effects were found on this measure. Not surprisingly, subjects perceived they had more control in the 75–0 contingency condition than in the 75–50 contingency condition, $F(1,39) = 6.48$, $p < .02$. In addition, high desire for control subjects felt they had more

TABLE 6-2. Mean Judgment of Perceived Control over Onset of Light

	High desire for control	Low desire for control
75–0 Condition (75% control)	64.11	50.36
75–50 Condition (25% control)	48.36	36.11

Note: Based on 101-point scale, with 0 = no control and 100 = complete control

control over the light than did low desire for control subjects, F $(1,39) = 4.93$, $p < .03$. However, there was no hint of an interaction effect, indicating that the high desire for control subjects perceived more control over the onset of the light than low desire for control subjects regardless of the real level of contingency.

The findings from this study are consistent with the notion that high desire for control people are so motivated to see themselves in control of events that, at least relative to low desire for control people, they distort the perception of how much control they have. It is important to interpret these findings in terms of the relative amount of perceived control high desire for control subjects and low desire for control subjects believed they had over the onset of the light. In truth, both types of subjects tended to overestimate their control in the 75–50 condition and underestimate their control in the 75–0 condition. However, observing the subjects' behavior and interviewing subjects after the experiment, it became clear that gauging one's control in this situation with just 40 trials is a rather difficult task.

It is tempting to argue that precisely because of this ambiguity individual differences in desire for control influenced the subjects' judgments of control in this experiment. That is, common sense might suggest that it would be difficult for high desire for control people to convince themselves that their control is excessive when the amount of control they have over the task is rather obvious. However, this seemingly apparent notion is contradicted by the results of the study reported next, as well as some research presented in Chapter 9, in which high desire for control subjects appear to convince themselves that they have some personal control over what should be obviously randomly determined events.

I demonstrated this phenomenon by utilizing a procedure developed by Langer and Roth (1975). These researchers had subjects guess heads or tails on each of 30 trials in a coin toss game. Predetermined feedback given after each trial informed all subjects that they had guessed correctly on 15 of the 30 trials, just as chance would dictate. However, some subjects received positive feedback in a descending sequence, such that they thought they had guessed correctly often at first, and made most of their incorrect guesses at the end. Other subjects received ascending positive feedback, such that they believed they had not guessed well at first, but toward the end of the sequence began to do noticeably better than chance. Langer and Roth found that subjects in the descending feedback condition demonstrated the greatest illusion of control. That is, these subjects thought they had done better, were more likely to attribute their correct guesses to ability, and predicted they would do better if they attempted the task again than did subjects in the other condition.

I reasoned that this illusion of control was partly the result of a need to see oneself in control, and therefore that high desire for control people would be more likely to show the illusion-of-control effect than low desire for control people (Burger, 1986). Consequently, I replicated the Langer and Roth (1975) procedures, but divided subjects in groups according to their desire for control. The pattern of results both supported my expectations and provided a surprise. First, as predicted, the greatest illusion of control was found among the high desire for control subjects in the descending condition. That is, when high desire for control subjects had a high percentage of correct guesses at the beginning of the sequence, they were more likely to attribute their correct guesses to their ability and predicted that they would do better on 100 more trials of this task than did the low desire for control subjects in this condition. It is particularly interesting to note that the subjects were college students who should have been able to see that the outcome of a coin toss game is chance determined and that the best guess of how they would do on 100 trials should be about 50. Nonetheless, whereas the low desire for control subjects in the descending condition gave an average guess of 50.45 for the next 100 trials, the high desire for control subjects said they would guess correctly an average of 59.87 times.

The surprise in these data came from subjects in the ascending feedback conditions. High desire for control subjects in this condition not only failed to demonstrate an illusion of control over the outcome of the coin toss, they showed the opposite effect. They tended to believe they had done worse than the low desire for control subjects at guessing on the 30 trials, that their correct answers were not the result of ability, and that they would do noticeably worse than chance if they had to guess on 100 more trials. In fact, these high desire for control subjects estimated that they would get only 42.36 correct guesses out of 100.

The data indicate that just as early success at guessing led the high desire for control people to believe that they were able to control the outcome of the game, early experiences at losing lead them to conclude that they were *not* able to exercise much control over the outcome. This finding suggests that high desire for control people are more likely than low desire for control people to analyze events in terms of whether they have control, and perhaps overinterpret information suggesting either they can or cannot control the event. On the other hand, who has control is not as important a question to people with a low desire for control. Unlike the high desire for control people, they do not tend to process information or analyze events in terms of a control filter.

This observation led to another question. Is this tendency by high desire for control people to interpret events in terms of control limited to the question of whether *they* can control the event? Or do high desire for control people also utilize this control filter when explaining other peoples' behavior, even when that behavior has no direct bearing on them? I explored this question in the experiment described in the next section.

ATTRIBUTIONS ABOUT OTHER PEOPLE'S CONTROL

I looked at how high desire for control people and low desire for control people perceive other people's control by modifying the coin toss experiment. Thirty-three undergraduates participated in this unpublished study with a confederate posing as a real subject. A rigged drawing assigned the confederate to the predictor role and the real subject to the evaluator role. The subject and the confederate each tossed coins on every trial. The confederate guessed match or no match before each toss, indicating whether he or she thought both coins would be the same (both heads, both tails) or not. The experimenter explained that the odds of being correct with a random guess were 50–50. The coin toss was rigged so that the confederate appeared to guess correctly 15 times out of 30, either in the descending or ascending order used in the earlier experiment (Burger, 1986). Following the trials, subjects filled out a questionnaire that asked, among other things, for them to estimate how many correct guesses the confederate made and how the confederate would do on 100 more trials.

The results from this experiment are shown in Table 6-3. Subjects did appear to use the descending–ascending sequence information to interpret the other person's performance on the task. Subjects who saw the confederate guess correctly at the beginning of the sequence thought the confederate had done better on the thirty trials, F (1,29) = 19.12, $p < .001$, and made higher estimates for the confederate's performance on 100 more trials, F (1,29) = 13.60, $p < .001$, than those in the ascending sequence condition. However, desire for control scores were not related to this effect. Although I examined these data several ways, I could find

TABLE 6-3. Estimates for the Confederate's Behavior

	Descending sequence		Ascending sequence	
	High desire for control	Low desire for control	High desire for control	Low desire for control
Correct guesses on 30 trials	17.38	17.89	12.44	13.71
Correct guesses on next 100 trials	58.75	55.22	42.44	44.29

no relationship between the subject's desire for control level and how he or she interpreted the confederate's performance.

Although it is difficult to interpret nonsignificant findings from this one experiment, the data raise some interesting questions. Essentially, both the high desire for control subjects and low desire for control subjects in this study acted like the high desire for control subjects in the earlier study describing their own behavior (Burger, 1986). Both were vulnerable to the illusion that the confederate was somehow able to influence the outcome of the coin toss in the descending sequence condition, and both tended to see the confederate as less able to control the coin toss than expected by chance in the ascending sequence condition. This finding raises the interesting possibility that low desire for control people somehow fail to interpret their own actions in terms of control, but do so when explaining other peoples' behavior.

Obviously, more research, including an experiment that examines attributions for both oneself and others, is needed. However, at this point it seems clear that desire for control may affect attributions we make for ourselves differently than attributions we make for other people. This point is also made in some of the research reviewed in the next section.

ATTRIBUTIONS FOR ONESELF RELATIVE TO OTHERS: UNREALISTIC OPTIMISM

Researchers consistently find that we see ourselves as less vulnerable to all sorts of negative life events than are others (Perloff & Fetzer, 1986; Weinstein, 1980, 1984, 1987). Subjects in these studies tend to rate their own chances of someday suffering from a heart attack, automobile accident, divorce, and so on as less than the chances of someone their own age and gender. Although some of these people no doubt are less likely to suffer these negative experiences, this cannot be true for everyone. Because the average ratings for the entire sample indicate a lack of perceived vulnerability, we can be certain that some distortion is going on.

Among the explanations for this unrealistic optimism effect is that people see themselves as relatively invulnerable to maintain a sense of personal control (Perloff & Fetzer, 1986; Weinstein, 1980). We do not want to admit that there is little we can do to prevent ourselves from falling victim to any of these problems. If this is the case, then we might expect high desire for control people and low desire for control people to differ in the extent to which they engage in unrealistic optimism. Admitting that there is nothing one can do to avoid cancer or a drinking problem should be more difficult for a high desire for control person to accept than for a person with a low desire for control. Consequently, high desire for control people should interpret their chances of escaping major life problems as relatively good compared to most people.

I tested this possibility in an unpublished study with 73 undergraduate subjects. Subjects rated on seven-point scales the extent to which they believed someday they would experience each of 10 negative life events (Perloff & Fetzer, 1986). Next, subjects rated on the same seven-point scales the extent to which the average person their age and gender would someday experience each event. As shown in Table 6-4, both high desire for control subjects and low desire for control subjects showed evidence of unrealistic optimism on several of the items, as indicated by their evaluation of themselves as less vulnerable than the average person. When I combined the magnitude of this effect from all ten items into one unrealistic optimism score, I found that high desire for control subjects were significantly more likely to see themselves as less vulnerable than were subjects with a low desire for control ($p < .05$). However, when examined separately, a statistically significant difference between high desire for control subjects and low desire for control subjects to engage in unrealistic optimism was found on only one item. High desire for

TABLE 6-4. Mean Estimates of Vulnerability to Negative Life Events

	High desire for control			Low desire for control		
	You	Average person	Dif.	You	Average person	Dif.
Cancer	3.19	3.72	0.53	2.87	3.29	0.42
Heart attack	2.94	3.50	0.56	3.00	3.37	0.37
Drinking problem	2.08	4.11	2.03	2.43	4.18	1.75
Divorce	2.31	4.36	2.05	2.70	4.51	1.81
Sexually transmitted disease	1.81	3.72	1.91	2.11	4.03	1.92
Mugged	2.92	3.58	0.66	3.39	3.82	0.43
Car accident	4.69	4.94	0.25	4.45	4.84	0.39
Hypertension	3.22	3.53	0.31	3.43	3.92	0.49
Nervous breakdown	2.08	3.31	1.23	2.54	3.16	0.62
Diabetes	2.36	3.06	0.70	2.16	2.73	0.57

Note: Vulnerability ratings on seven-point scales, with 1 = not at all likely and 7 = extremely likely

control subjects were significantly more likely to engage in unrealistic optimism when asked about a nervous breakdown than were subjects with a low desire for control. This is an interesting finding in that *nervous breakdown* seems to connote by definition a loss of control over oneself, something a high desire for control person is highly motivated to avoid.

Another way of looking at the unrealistic optimism data is to compare the extent to which high desire for control people and low desire for control people saw themselves as vulnerable, regardless of their perceived vulnerability for other people. When I compared these ratings I found that the high desire for control subjects generally gave themselves lower vulnerability estimates than did subjects with a low desire for control ($p < .05$).

A similar finding was reported by Drake (1987). Undergraduate subjects in this study were asked to rate the likelihood that they and other people would someday experience each of four events, some of them negative (divorce, attempt suicide) and some positive (travel to Europe, own your own home). An overall optimism score from these responses was correlated with DC Scale scores taken four weeks earlier. Drake found a significant positive correlation, $r = .38$, indicating that high desire for control subjects expressed more optimism than subjects with a low desire for control.

Thus, although both high desire for control people and low desire for control people engage in unrealistic optimism, there is some evidence that high desire for control people do this more than low desire for control people. This is consistent with the notion that maintaining a sense of relative invulnerability allows a person to retain a sense of control over potentially tragic experiences. I could also speculate that high desire for control people will be particularly likely to see themselves as less vulnerable than others when thinking about an experience with a serious loss of control, such as a nervous breakdown. The findings from this study also are consistent with the findings from the illusion of control studies, which indicate that people with a high desire for control are so motivated to see themselves in control of events that they often distort their perception of control to satisfy this need.

SUMMARY

Desire for control appears to be related to how people process information and how they explain the causes of events in many ways. Compared to people with a low desire for control, high desire for control people are more active pursuers of information that will help them understand the causes of their own and other people's behavior. High desire for control people attend to attributionally relevant information, ask questions that help them make accurate attributions, and make relatively more attributions for the causes of their own behaviors. High desire for control people also are more likely than low desire for control people to attribute their behavior to causes that allow them to maintain a sense of control. Thus, high desire for control people are more likely to use internal attributions, such as ability and effort, to explain the outcome of their endeavors.

Despite this increased effort to come to an understanding of why things turn out the way they do, in some situations high desire for control people may be less accurate in their attributions than people with a low desire for control. This is because high desire for control people are more likely to attend to control-relevant information. At times this tendency leads to inaccurate conclusions, such as when the high desire for control people believe they have more or less control over a chance determined event than objectively justified. Interestingly, this tendency to overinterpret control-relevant information was not found in one study in which high desire for control people made attributions for another person's outcomes. It may be that people with a high desire for control are more interested in answering the question "Can I control this?" rather than "Can he or she control this?" In other words, high desire for control people may use their control filter to process information primarily when understanding the causes of behavior relevant to their own sense of control.

CHAPTER 7

WELL-BEING, ADJUSTMENT, AND HEALTH

Inevitably, discussions about desire for control get around to the question of whether people with a high desire for control or people with a low desire for control are better adjusted and happier. Not surprisingly, I typically find that high desire for control people say that they are better off psychologically, while low desire for control people maintain the opposite. Although a case can be made for both of these positions, the research reviewed in this chapter indicates that a simple answer to the question probably is not possible. As I will discuss at the end of the chapter, most likely both high desire for control people and low desire for control people can be well-adjusted and happy, depending upon many other factors.

Examining well-being and personal adjustment also requires looking at many different variables that make up an individual's ability to function effectively in society. Certainly how well high desire for control people and low desire for control people do at school and in their jobs is relevant. Similarly, the quality of and satisfaction in one's interpersonal relationships play an important role in personal adjustment. Thus, the research covered in Chapter 3 (interpersonal relations) and Chapter 5 (achievement) is relevant in a discussion of well-being. The research covered in this chapter deals with more direct indices of well-being. That is, I will examine research relating desire for control to anxiety, measures of general well-being, and coping strategies. In addition, I look at how a high desire for control might be a sign or symptom of various psychological disorders. Finally, I examine evidence tying desire for control to health and health behaviors.

DESIRE FOR CONTROL AND ANXIETY

Two reasonable hypotheses spring to mind concerning the relationship between desire for control and anxiety. First, we can speculate that a high desire for control will be associated with increased levels of anxiety. Research covered in Chapter 5 indicates that high desire for control people are more driven to achieve, have higher ambitions, are more competitive, and are more responsive to challenges than people with a low desire for control. Although these reactions often lead to increased performance and achievement, the down side is that in the extreme these people sound anything but relaxed and stressfree. We might guess that a businessman or businesswoman with a high desire for control is the one who puts in extra time at work, takes work home, and is driven to rise to the top of the organization. He or she is the person who always tackles that next challenging task, only to take on an even more challenging task when the first one is conquered.

Further, the sad truth is that the world is not set up to always satisfy a high need for control. Inevitably, business downslides, strong competition, personal errors, lack of ability, and more demands than allotable time lead even the best of us to acknowledge that we cannot control some of the situations we encounter in life. Lazarus and Folkman (1984) define *stress* in terms of a person's perception that the demands of the situation are "taxing or exceeding" his or her resources to deal with the situation effectively. Because many of the demands on high desire for control people are self-imposed, it is reasonable to predict that high desire for control will be associated with higher levels of stress and anxiety.

However, the opposite prediction also is possible. Because they achieve more, high desire for control people may feel better able to deal with the events in their lives than people with a low desire for control. When problems occur, high desire for control people more often take direct action to resolve the issue or diffuse the threat. Some research indicates that such active, problem-solving efforts typically are more effective for long-term stress reduction than trying to deal with emotional reactions to the stressor or trying to avoid or deny the problem (Suls & Fletcher, 1985). Further, taking action, even when ineffective, may provide high desire for control people with the feeling that they can deal with a problem situation rather than become resigned and helpless.

Thus, there are reasons to suspect that either a high desire for control or a low desire for control will be associated with higher levels of anxiety. Two kinds of research data help to resolve this issue. I look first at how desire for control correlates with various individual difference measures of anxiety. Next, I examine research on how high desire for control people and low desire for control people react to situational manipulations of potential stressors.

CORRELATIONS WITH INDIVIDUAL DIFFERENCE MEASURES

What is the relationship between DC Scale scores and measures of anxiety? In an initial investigation of this question, I asked undergraduates to complete the DC Scale, the Spielberger State Anxiety Scale, and the Spielberger Trait Anxiety Scale (Spielberger, Gorsuch, & Lushene, 1970). The State Anxiety Scale asks respondents to describe the extent to which they currently are experiencing various symptoms of anxiety (e.g., "I am tense," "I feel nervous"). The trait scale asks test takers to respond to similar items, but to indicate the extent to which they generally have these experiences.

Although only 41 undergraduates were tested in this unpublished study, I found evidence for a negative relationship between desire for control scores and trait anxiety ($r = -.37$) and between desire for control and state anxiety ($r = -.22$). Thus, the higher the students' level of desire for control, the less anxiety they reported experiencing at the time of the testing and in their lives generally.

In a follow-up study, I administered the DC Scale and several additional measures, including the Interaction Anxiousness Scale (Leary, 1983), to 74 undergraduates. The Interaction Anxiousness Scale was designed to measure the extent to which people generally experience anxiety in social interactions. The results of this unpublished study again uncovered a significant negative relationship, $r = -.38$, with lower desire for control scores associated with higher levels of interaction anxiety. A similar relationship was reported in a pair of studies by Schönbach (1990). He gave a German translation of the DC Scale and a measure of social anxiety to groups of German citizens. Consistent with the results from my research, Schönbach found correlations between the two measures of $-.48$ and $-.24$ for his male subjects, and $-.43$ and $-.40$ for female subjects. Similarly, Thompson (1990) reports correlations of $-.25$ and $-.50$ between the DC Scale and measures of interaction anxiety and social anxiety, respectively.

Santos and Burger (1988) used a slightly different methodology to examine this relationship. Undergraduates completed the DC Scale along with a package of measures at the beginning of the study. Twenty-nine of these undergraduates also completed the Spielberger State Anxiety Scale at the end of each day for 14 consecutive days. We summed the 14 scores to determine an overall anxiety level score for the two-week period. When this score was correlated with the earlier DC Scale score, a significant negative correlation was found, $r = -.38$.

In summary, when we look at simple correlations between desire for control and various self-report measures of anxiety, a fairly clear pattern emerges. As shown in Table 7-1, people who score high on the DC Scale tend to report less anxiety in their lives. It would be tempting to conclude from these data either that high desire for control people are better able to avoid or overcome sources of stress than are low desire for control people, or that something about a low desire for control leads to increased stress. However, such a conclusion would be premature for a number of reasons.

First, this type of correlational data raises questions about the direction of causality. That is, we could also explain these data in terms of anxiety leading to a lower desire for control, or that some third variable is responsible for both the high desire for control and low anxiety. For example, it is possible that experience with a series of stressful events, such as loss of job security, relationship troubles, and financial troubles, probably would lead to increased anxiety. But these same conditions could also cause a person to feel like giving up, that nothing he or she does will do any good. Second, interpreting these data requires that we accept that high desire for control people and low desire for control people report their anxiety levels with similar accuracy. Third, even if high desire for control people correctly report that they experience less anxiety than low desire for control people, this may be because they are better able to deal with the stress that they encounter, not because they

TABLE 7-1. Correlations between DC Scale Scores and Measures of Anxiety

Source	Scale	N	r	p
Burger (unpublished)	Spielberger Trait Anxiety	41	-.37	.02
Burger (unpublished)	Spielberger Trait Anxiety	41	-.22	.17
Burger (unpublished)	Leary Social Anxiety	74	-.38	.001
Schönbach (1990)	Social Anxiety	92 (males)	-.48	.01
Schönbach (1990)	Social Anxiety	45 (males)	-.24	.10
Schönbach (1990)	Social Anxiety	93 (females)	-.43	.01
Schönbach (1990)	Social Anxiety	45 (females)	-.40	.01
Santos and Burger (1988)	Spielberger State Anxiety (two-week average)	29	-.38	.04
Thompson (1990)	Interaction Anxiety	193	-.25	.001
Thompson (1990)	Social Anxiety	107	-.50	.001

have less stress in their lives. Finally, as described next, these data deal with general measures of stress and anxiety. It is possible that a high desire for control leads to an increase, rather than a decrease, in anxiety under more specific circumstances.

REACTIONS TO UNCONTROLLABLE SITUATIONS

One explanation for why high desire for control people typically report less anxiety than people with a low desire for control is that they may structure their lives so that their need for control is met most of the time. However, these high desire for control people might still have more difficulty than low desire for control people in dealing with the inevitable situation over which they can exercise little control. If that is the case, then both hypotheses concerning the desire for control–anxiety relationship might be correct. High desire for control people may experience more anxiety, but they may deal with it more effectively as well.

This possibility is suggested by data from several investigations. One of these studies dealt with an interesting phenomenon sometimes encountered by clinical psychologists using relaxation training with their clients. Although the vast majority of people going through relaxation training report at least some increase in relaxation following the treatment, a noticeable minority of clients report that they are more anxious following the treatment than before (Heide & Borkovec, 1983). Heide and Borkovec (1983) speculate that one reason for this counterintuitive reaction is that the subjects may have feared they were losing control.

To test this possibility, Braith, McCullough, and Bush (1988) identified a group of clients who showed increases in anxiety following a 30-minute relaxation training session on at least two of the following measures: self-reported anxiety, heart rate, tonic skin conductance, and phasic skin conductance. These subjects were compared on a number of personality dimensions with those subjects who did not show increased anxiety. The researchers found only one personality scale on which the two groups differed—the DC Scale. The increased-anxiety subjects averaged higher DC Scale scores than the comparison subjects.

This finding is consistent with the reasoning outlined earlier for why a high desire for control might be related to an increase in anxiety. High desire for control people may be particularly vulnerable to anxiety when experiencing a situation over which they feel they have no control. In this case, even the relatively nonthreatening relaxation training appears to have met the criteria. High desire for control clients may have been unwilling to relinquish control to the therapist. The relaxation training thus became another source of anxiety, resulting in the opposite effect for which it was intended.

A similar line of reasoning can be used to explain the results of a recent study by Ryland and Levy (1988). These researchers surveyed 245 employees in financial aid offices in 25 postsecondary schools. The subjects included clerks, technicians, counselors, assistant directors, associate directors, and directors. Each was administered a work–stress scale developed specifically for the study. The scale asked about stress in dealing with management, workload, clients, rules and regulations, and so on. The subjects also completed the DC Scale.

The correlation between desire for control and stress for the overall sample was low and nonsignificant, $r = .09$. However, a different picture emerged when correlations were calculated separately for male and female employees. The males showed virtually no relationship between desire for control and work-related stress, $r = -.01$. However, a small but significant correlation was found for the female subjects, $r = .17$, $p < .02$. Thus, the higher the desire for control level in the female employees, the more work stress they experienced.

Why might this be so? One possibility is that the women with a high desire for control experienced a great deal of frustration in satisfying that need. Many of the women in the sample may have had more difficulty than the men in getting what they wanted in their interactions with supervisors or clients. These women may have experienced a lack of respect, lack of opportunity, a glass ceiling for career advancement, and other problems not typically encountered by their male counterparts. The men who did not experience these obstacles and the women who did not have a high need to exercise control over their work environment may not have experienced the levels of stress at work that these high desire for control women did. Although highly speculative, this interpretation is consistent with the notion that high desire for control people may be more susceptible than others to anxiety when their need for control is not satisfied.

Yet another piece of evidence to support the prediction that a high desire for control is sometimes associated with higher anxiety comes from two experiments by Lawler, Schmied, Armstead, and Lacy (1990). These researchers looked at several physiological reactivity measures while undergraduate females worked on a mildly stressful reaction time task. Although desire for control alone did not predict increased reactivity to the challenging task, Lawler et al. found a fairly consistent pattern when looking at the interaction between desire for control and Type A behavior pattern. Subjects who scored high in both desire for control and

Type A personality showed significantly stronger physiological reactions to the task than subjects in any of the other groups.

The investigators interpreted these findings to suggest that desire for control may be a critical link between Type A personality and physiological reactivity in women. Some research has failed to demonstrate the type of physiological reaction in Type A undergraduate women that is typically found in Type A undergraduate males. This difference may have to do with the slightly higher desire for control score sometimes found among male subjects (see Chapter 2). The findings also suggest that even mildly stressful situations, such as the reaction time task used in these experiments, can produce anxiety in some high desire for control people.

What can we conclude about the relationship between desire for control and anxiety? The best interpretation of the available data seems to be that whereas high desire for control people are more apt to find certain situations potentially stressful than are low desire for control people, they generally seem better able to (or report they are better able to) deal with sources of anxiety. In fact, I might even speculate that high desire for control people are more likely to place themselves in potentially threatening situations, such as high-pressure business deals, but only to the extent that they feel they are able to control them. As long as high desire for control people are able to structure their worlds to avoid highly stressful *un*controllable situations, they probably fare better than people with a low desire for control. Thus, a high desire for control may be something of a two-edged sword, helping to deal with potential sources of anxiety most of the time, but perhaps making one vulnerable to excessive anxiety when efforts at control fail.

DESIRE FOR CONTROL AND WELL-BEING

Although the presence or absence of anxiety is an important component of personal adjustment and well-being, we can expand the question to ask who is generally happier and more content—high desire for control people or low desire for control people? Although more research is needed, the data available to date tend to point to the same conclusion.

Some initial data for answering this question came from an unpublished study I conducted. I administered three general measures of well-being and the DC Scale to 74 undergraduates. The students completed the Bradburn Affect Scales (Bradburn, 1969), which provides measures of positive and negative affect. Test takers are asked if they have experienced each of five positive and five negative affective states in the past few weeks. In addition, students completed the Rosenberg Self-Esteem Scale (Rosenberg, 1965).

An interesting pattern of results emerged in this study. A strong positive correlation was found between desire for control and positive affect, $r = .40$, $p < .001$. Interestingly, however, there was no correlation between desire for control and negative affect, $r = -.03$. I also found a strong positive correlation between desire for control and self-esteem, $r = .40$, $p < .001$. Thus, the higher one's desire for control, the higher the self-esteem.

The positive correlation between desire for control and self-esteem is also found in research reported by other investigators. Daubman (1990) found a positive correlation of .27 ($p < .01$) between the DC Scale and Rosenberg Self-Esteem Scale. Similarly, Thompson (1990) reports a correlation of .49 ($p < .001$) between desire for control and a measure of self-esteem. Finally, Schönbach (1990) had subjects complete a German version of the DC Scale and a measure of self-dissatisfaction in five independent studies. He reports correlations between the two measures broken down by gender that range from −.20 to −.45 for male subjects and −.19 to −.54 for female subjects. The correlations are significant at least at the .05 level in eight of the ten cases, and are significant at the .10 level in the two other cases. In all cases, people scoring high in desire for control scored low on self-*dis*satisfaction. Thus, this research also finds that people with a high desire for control score higher than low desire for control people on measures of self-esteem.

Yet another indicator of the link between desire for control and well-being is found in the work of Snyder and his colleagues on the concept of hope (Snyder, 1989; Snyder et al., 1989; Snyder et al., 1991). According to Snyder, a sense of hope provides people with the energy to work toward achieving their goals and with the development of plans to meet those goals. In this way, we are said to maintain a sense of self associated with good psychological health (Snyder, 1989). Snyder and his colleagues have developed a 14-item and an 8-item Hope Scale to measure individual differences in the hope motive. They also have identified two subscale scores, one assessing the goal-directed energy component of hope motivation (Agency subscale) and one assessing the plans to meet goals component (Pathways subscale).

When Snyder compared scores on the 14-item Hope Scale with scores on the DC Scale, he found a significant correlation of .45 (Snyder, 1989). An even higher correlation of .54 was found between the DC Scale and the 8-item scale (Snyder, et al., 1989). In addition, the DC Scale correlated significantly with both the Agency ($r = .43$) and Pathways ($r = .49$) subscales of the 8-item measure in this last study. These findings fit well with Snyder's model of psychological health and help to explain one of the links between desire for control and well-being. Consistent with the reasoning presented earlier, people with a high desire for control appear more likely than low desire for control people generally to know what they want and to go after it. Because they believe they can reach these goals (that is, they are full of hope), they maintain a more adaptive and healthy sense of self than those with a low desire for control.

In summary, the Desire for Control Scale tends to correlate positively with individual difference measures of general well-being. When combined with the consistent pattern of correlations found between desire for control and measures of anxiety, there is strong evidence that a high desire for control is associated with psychological health and good personal adjustment. However, other evidence indicates that high desire for control people at least occasionally create more stress for themselves than people with a low desire for control. This suggests that high desire for control people are able to deal with these incidents and get themselves back on track relatively effectively. How they do this will be examined in the next section.

COPING WITH STRESS

I suggested earlier that high desire for control people and low desire for control people may differ in the way they handle stress. In particular, high desire for control people should choose a course of action that best meets their need to feel in control of the situation. Thus, wherever possible, they probably prefer to take direct action to resolve the issue. In addition, people with a high desire for control probably prefer to deal with the problem themselves, rather than depending on others or relying on resources outside of their control.

I examined this prediction as part of a series of laboratory experiments (Burger, McWard, & LaTorre, 1989). Subjects in these experiments were told that the experimenter needed to take a blood sample and that a few drops of their blood would be obtained by pricking the tip of a finger with a sanitized lancet. Pilot testing had revealed that subjects found this request to be moderately stressful. Subjects were given the choice of having the experimenter take the blood sample or of pricking their own finger. Several previous studies found that about 70% of the subjects opted for the experimenter to administer that blood sampling. That is, most subjects felt that the least stressful way to deal with this unpleasant task was to relinquish control to someone who was probably better qualified than they were. For the majority of people, retaining a sense of personal control over the event was not as important as seeing that it was done well.

But what about people with a high desire for control? Not only is the prospect of relinquishing control over an important event stressful for these people, they may also believe that the best way to deal with a potentially threatening situation is to take action and do something themselves. People with a high desire for control are likely to maintain that giving up personal control over a stressful event is the least effective way to see that things turn out as they wish.

Consistent with this reasoning, we divided subjects in one experiment into halves based on desire for control. As expected, the vast majority of the subjects with a low desire for control preferred that the experimenter take the blood sample (78.3%), whereas fewer than half of the high desire for control subjects opted to relinquish control to the experimenter (45%). In this situation the high desire for control subjects were more likely than low desire for control subjects to adopt a direct action, personal control type of strategy for dealing with the moderately stressful situation.

Another way to examine this hypothesis is to look at the types of coping strategies typically employed by high desire for control people and low desire for control people. A great deal of research finds that people tend to develop characteristic strategies for dealing with problems and sources of stress. Some researchers have divided the many strategies people employ into those that focus on solving the problem and those that attempt to deal with the emotional distress (Lazarus & Folkman, 1984; Suls & Fletcher, 1985). We can also look at the extent to which people engage in active efforts to deal with the situation versus passive or indirect methods. For example, Holahan and Moos (1987) divided the various strategies people reported using to deal with a recent problem into active–cognitive strategies (active efforts to construct thoughts to help cope with the problem), active–behavioral strategies (active efforts to do something to change the situation), and avoidance strategies (trying to keep the problem out of awareness).

If the reasoning described above is correct, I would expect high desire for control people to be more likely than low desire for control people to take active efforts to deal with a stressful situation, and to do this in a way that allows them to feel as if they have overcome the problem themselves. As the research on attributional activity reviewed in Chapter 6 suggests, high desire for control people may spend a large amount of time gathering all the information they can to deal with the problem most effectively.

I conducted a relatively simple study to look into differences in the types of coping strategies typically used by high desire for control people and low desire for control people. I adopted the procedures described by Holahan and Moos (1987) in this unpublished study. Seventy-

four undergraduates were asked to think about the most important problem they faced during the past year, either one that had been resolved
or one that was ongoing. I then presented subjects with a list of the 32
coping strategies identified by Holahan and Moos. These included some
active–cognitive, active–behavioral, and avoidance strategies. Subjects indicated the extent to which they had used each of the strategies on a 0
to 3 scale, with 3 indicating they had used the strategy fairly often to
deal with a problem.

I first looked at the strategies used most frequently by high desire
for control subjects and low desire for control subjects. Table 7-2 lists
the strategies that received mean ratings of 2.0 or better for each of
the desire for control groups. A look at the table provides an interesting picture of the different ways high desire for control people and low
desire for control people go about dealing with their problems. Because
I asked subjects to select the most important problem they had faced
that year, it is not surprising that both groups reported spending a lot
of time going over the situation in their minds. However, beyond
this similarity the two lists paint different pictures. As expected, high
desire for control subjects were more likely to collect information
and consider many options for dealing with the situation. They also
generally seemed to rely on more active strategies, such as trying harder
to make things work and obtaining information and advice from friends.

TABLE 7-2. Mean Ratings of Coping Strategies Most Often Used by
High Desire for Control Subjects and Low Desire for Control Subjects

	Mean rating
High Desire for Control Subjects	
I went over the situation in my mind trying to understand it	2.67
I tried to find out more about the situation	2.64
I considered several alternatives for handling the situation	2.36
I talked with a friend about the problem	2.33
I knew what had to be done and tried harder to make things work	2.22
I made a promise to myself that things would be different next time	2.22
I tried to see the positive side of the situation	2.14
I drew on my past experience	2.03
Low Desire for Control Subjects	
I went over the situation in my mind to try to understand it	2.68
I considered several alternatives for handling the situation	2.18
I let my feelings out somehow	2.08
I prayed for guidance and/or strength	2.05
I took things one day at a time	2.05

Note: Means based on a four-point scale, with 3 = used fairly often, 0 = did not use at all

On the other hand, low desire for control subjects were less likely than high desire for control subjects to cite active strategies or to seek out helpful information.

I also compared high desire for control subjects with low desire for control subjects for their use of specific items. High desire for control subjects were significantly more likely than subjects with a low desire for control to use five of the strategies ($p < .05$). These are presented in Table 7-3. The items in the table again indicate that high desire for control people are more likely to take active efforts to deal with their problems than are people with a low desire for control. In no case did low desire for control subjects report using a strategy more often than high desire for control subjects.

Although the effectiveness of a given strategy depends on many situational variables, there appears to be general agreement among researchers that active strategies are more effective in the long run than avoidant strategies, and problem-focused strategies are more effective than those that attempt to deal only with emotional distress (Suls & Fletcher, 1985). If this is the case, then we can make the argument, still in need of much research support, that high desire for control people generally are more effective in coping with their problems than people with a low desire for control. Because they are more likely to gather information and consider alternative solutions and then take active steps to resolve the problem, high desire for control people may do a better job than low desire for control people of handling the large and small difficulties that life throws our way. This analysis also helps to explain why high desire for control people generally report lower levels of anxiety in their daily lives and score higher on measures of well-being than people with a low desire for control.

TABLE 7-3. Mean Ratings of Strategies Used More Often by
High Desire for Control Subjects than Low Desire for Control Subjects

Strategy	High desire for control	Low desire for control
I tried to find out more about the situation	2.64	1.97
I talked with a friend about the problem	2.33	1.95
I drew on my past experiences	2.03	1.61
I knew what had to be done and tried harder to make things work	2.22	1.87
I made a promise to myself that things would be different next time	2.22	1.82

HIGH DESIRE FOR CONTROL
AND PSYCHOLOGICAL PROBLEMS

The research reviewed thus far suggests a positive link between a high desire for control and well-being. However, it is important to emphasize that this work has been conducted with groups, often undergraduates, who on the whole show few outward signs of disorders or dysfunction. Although little direct research has been conducted on this question, there are reasons to suspect that on occasion a high need for control may be symptomatic of a deeper psychological disorder, and that this high need for control may also contribute to problem behavior. This possibility does not negate the positive link between a high desire for control and well-being described above. However, it probably would be incorrect to assume that desire for control and well-being are synonymous.

This point can best be illustrated with the work of many researchers on the very large number of adult children of alcoholics (cf. West & Prinz, 1987). One of the most persistent observations of psychologists working in this area is the clients' high need for control and autonomy (Berkowitz & Perkins, 1988; Brown, 1988). Children growing up with one or more alcoholic parents live in a home characterized by chaos and unpredictability. These children often learn that they have little control over what happens to them or the members of their family (Prewett, Spence, & Chaknis, 1981). They attempt to cope with this extremely uncontrollable situation by trying to exercise as much control over themselves and others as possible (Brown, 1988). The high need for control that develops as a defensive adaptation in childhood remains a part of the personality of the adult long after he or she has moved out of the house. These children and adults believe exercising control provides a means to avoid or limit the feelings of vulnerability and unpredictability that remain from the earlier experiences. Some adult children of alcoholics also fear that they may lose control and begin to act like their alcoholic parents.

The high need for control among adult children of alcoholics is not only symptomatic of deeper problems, but can often lead to other difficulties. In particular, this high need for control often makes it difficult for these adults to establish intimate interpersonal relationships (Brown, 1988). Adult children of alcoholics may be reluctant to share feelings, risk the vulnerability of intimacy, or trust others. Therapy for adult children of alcoholics often includes an effort to help clients reduce their emphasis on control.

It is also possible that a high desire for control can lead to problem behaviors. That is, there are socially appropriate and inappropriate ways of expressing and satisfying a high desire for control. One interesting example of what may be an inappropriate expression of a high desire for control is suggested in a study by Breslow (1987). Breslow used magazine advertisements and contacted relevant clubs and businesses to locate a sample of sexual sadomasochists. He divided his sample into those who limited their sadomasochistic behavior to the dominant role (sadists), those who limited themselves to the submissive role (masochists), or those who sometimes engaged in both types of behavior (versatiles). Subjects were administered the DC Scale and were specifically cautioned to avoid thinking of the questions in a sexual manner, but rather to answer in reference to their everyday behavior.

Breslow found significant differences between each of the three groups. The sadists ($M = 117.4$) scored significantly higher on the scale than the versatiles ($M = 105.9$), who scored significantly higher than the masochists ($M = 96.9$). The direction of these differences makes sense. Dominating another individual during sexual encounters is a form of exercising control, whereas allowing oneself to be dominated is tantamount to relinquishing control.

Unfortunately, Breslow did not administer the scale to a matched control group, thus making it difficult to gauge how these scores would compare to those of comparable people who do not engage in sadomasochistic behavior. However, it is intriguing that the mean score for the sadists is between one and two standard deviations above the mean score typically found for people in similar age groups. This suggests that for a few people sadistic sexual behavior might become an outlet for a high need for control. Of course, it is also possible that the high desire for control and preference for sadism are both the result of another aspect of these people's personalities, such as a high need for dominance or power. It also is not clear that this behavior should be labeled as deviant or abnormal, although it clearly falls out of the range of typical sexual behavior. However, the data suggest that a high desire for control carries with it the possibility that, at least for some, the need will be satisfied in unusual ways.

HEALTH AND HEALTH BEHAVIOR

Ever since researchers first found a link between the Type A personality pattern and health a few decades ago, a growing number of psychologists have been concerned with the relationship between personality and physical health. In addition to Type A personality, health and health behaviors have been associated with such personality vari-

ables as optimism (Scheier & Carver, 1985), psychological hardiness (Kobasa, 1979), and locus of control (Strickland, 1978). A case can also be
made that desire for control may be related to health. Some researchers
have examined this relationship with scales specifically designed to
measure the extent to which people prefer to control health-care processes and health-related decisions (Smith, Wallston, Wallston, Forsberg,
& King, 1984). Although examining this domain-specific desire for control has proven useful in predicting many health-related behaviors, there
are reasons to suspect that a person's general desire for control level also
is related to health concerns and behavior. As is often the case, when it
comes to one's health, a high desire for control may be beneficial as well
as harmful.

HEALTH HABITS AND HEALTH-RELATED BEHAVIORS

My initial hypothesis was that high desire for control people would
be in better health generally than low desire for control people. I expected this because high desire for control people should be more likely
than low desire for control people to take steps to keep themselves
in good health and to deal effectively with health problems when they
occur. Rather than relinquish the state of their health to health-care professionals or to fate, high desire for control people should be motivated
to do what they can to prevent and overcome health problems. There
is widespread acceptance these days that there is much we can do to
keep ourselves healthy. I reasoned that high desire for control people
would be more motivated than people with a low desire for control
to take the necessary actions to keep themselves in good health. Thus,
high desire for control people should be more likely to eat well, exercise regularly, and take safety precautions because they believe these
behaviors will lead to better health. I conducted three short studies to
test this hypothesis.

In an initial examination of this question, I asked 66 undergraduates
to indicate the extent to which they engaged in six behaviors associated
with the prevention of health problems and accidents. I asked subjects
in this unpublished study how many hours per week they spent exercising, how many hours they spent per week participating in organized
athletic games, how often they used their seat belt, to what extent they
tried to avoid cancer-related foods, if they have checked their breasts/tes-
ticles for lumps at any time in the past 12 months, and if they considered
themselves to be overweight. The subjects also completed the DC Scale.
Significant differences emerged on only two of the six items, but these
were in the predicted direction. High desire for control subjects spent

more time playing in organized athletic activities than subjects with a low desire for control ($p < .058$). In addition, whereas 18.8% of the high desire for control subjects said that they were overweight, 41.2% of the low desire for control subjects described themselves this way ($p < .05$).

Another study looked at how desire for control was related to health behavior and experiences with minor health problems over a 14-day period (Santos & Burger, 1988). We gave 30 undergraduates the DC Scale and the Self Care Inventory (Pardine, Napoli & Dytell, 1983). The latter scale was designed to assess the extent to which people typically engage in several health-related behaviors (for example, alcohol consumption, diet, hand washing). In addition, subjects completed a daily inventory for the next 14 days. At the end of each day, subjects indicated whether they had experienced any of 19 minor health problems that day (for example, headache, coughing, diarrhea). The scores from the 14 inventories were totaled to produce an overall health score for the two-week period.

The results indicated that higher desire for control scores were positively related to health-promoting behaviors ($r = .27$). However, desire for control was not related to the number of minor health problems ($r = -.10$). Thus, as in the earlier studies, high desire for control subjects engaged in better health habits than subjects with a low desire for control. However, we found no evidence that these different health habits translated into better health for high desire for control subjects. Naturally, one of the difficulties in interpreting this last finding is the way we measured health. The relationship between the kinds of minor problems we examined and serious health concerns is questionable, especially among the relatively healthy population of undergraduates we looked at.

Finally, I speculated that desire for control might be related to health to the extent that it affected drug and alcohol use. I reasoned that high desire for control people would be more reluctant than low desire for control people to experiment with drugs or to drink to excess. Drug use and alcohol abuse might be seen as instances of relinquishing control, something the high desire for control person is reluctant to do (Burger et al., 1989). Indeed, drug education programs often emphasize how users fall under the drug's influence and people who drink heavily often talk about how they lost control over what they were doing or do not even remember what happened to them. Such experiences should be more threatening to high desire for control people than to people with a low desire for control.

The only relevant data I have on this question come from an unpublished study conducted with a colleague, Larry Young. We surveyed 53 undergraduates about their drinking habits (the study was conducted in a state with a legal drinking age of 18 at the time). We also presented subjects with nine scenarios (for example, a first date, a job interview, a party with friends) and asked subjects to indicate how much they would probably drink in each situation. Unfortunately, we found no correlation between desire for control scores and the average amount of alcohol the students consumed, $r = -.07$, or the amount they said they would probably drink when we totaled the nine scenario scores, $r = .02$. Again, one problem with interpreting these data is the nature of the sample we used. Although there may have been a few problem drinkers in the sample, the majority of subjects reported moderate to light drinking habits. Thus, while we found no evidence that desire for control was related to social drinking behavior, how desire for control relates to problem drinking remains an open question.

Although much more work needs to be done in this area, the available data provide at least some evidence to support the idea that high desire for control people and low desire for control people differ in their approach to their health and health-related behaviors. As they do in other areas of their lives, high desire for control people may take a more active effort to control their health than do low desire for control people. Caution needs to be used in interpreting these data, however. In particular, the studies to date have all dealt with relatively healthy undergraduates and have been limited by the self-report nature of the data. Nonetheless, while high desire for control people help themselves with better health habits, some data suggest that for some people a high desire for control might also be potentially hazardous to one's health. This research is described in the next section.

PHYSIOLOGICAL REACTIVITY

There is some evidence that high desire for control people are more inclined to a strong physiological reaction to stress than those with a low need for control. Perhaps such findings should not be surprising, in that high desire for control people generally respond with greater effort to challenges and threats to their perception of control. However, this difference in physiological responsiveness may also have implications for health. That is, it is possible that high desire for control people and low desire for control people have different responses to stress not only in terms of coping strategies, but also in terms of how they respond physiologically. Although the leap is a large one at this time, it is possible that these different physiological responses could eventually have an effect on one's health.

Several investigations have suggested a relationship between perceptions of personal control and heart attacks (Binik, 1985; Engel, 1971). Although many stressors have been associated with heart attacks, one that sometimes surfaces in this research is a perceived inability to control an important stressful event and/or a sudden loss of control over such an event. If a stressful loss of control is related to cardiovascular problems, and if high desire for control people are more likely than low desire for control people to exhibit such a response, then high desire for control people might be at higher risk for such problems than people with a low desire for control.

Indirect evidence for this connection comes from a study by Lawler *et al.* (1990). These investigators found that Type A women who also were high in desire for control had the largest increases in heart rate of any of their groups when experiencing mild stress. Although a slight increase in heart rate is far different than a heart attack, the finding does support the notion that high desire for control people have different physiological reactions to stressors than people with a low desire for control.

A more direct examination of the link between desire for control and cardiovascular problems was conducted by Hatton *et al.* (1989). These researchers examined patients who either had a history of ventricular fibrillation or had experienced clinical episodes of ventricular tachycardia. In nonmedical terms, these were patients with a health history suggesting they were at high risk for a sudden, lethal heart attack.

Hatton *et al.* (1989) administered electrical stimulation to the patients' hearts in an effort to produce ventricular arrhythmias (unusual heart beats). Past research has indicated that patients showing the arrhythmias with this procedure are at much higher risk for another heart attack than those not showing this reaction. The researchers used several personality measures to predict reaction to the electrical stimulation procedure. They looked at Type A Behavior Pattern, components of Type A personality (Speed and Impatience, Job Involvement, Hard Driving), three subscales from the Multidimensional Health Locus of Control Scales (Internal, Chance, Powerful Others), and, of course, desire for control. They found that only desire for control was able to predict reaction to the electrical stimulation procedure. DC Scale scores correlated highly with the severity of the arrhythmia response ($r = .55$). Further, patients who showed the high-risk arrhythmia response had significantly higher DC Scale scores than those who did not show this response. Finally, the researchers noted that desire for control was negatively related to systolic blood pressure prior to the experimental procedure ($r = -.74$).

Naturally, interpretation of these data must be tentative until further studies of this kind are conducted. However, Hatton *et al.* (1989) suggest that "arousal of the sympathetic nervous system, perhaps caused by an exaggerated need for environmental control, may make . . . desire for control [a] risk factor for sudden cardiac death" (p. 627). It is interesting to note that the researchers found the high desire for control subjects were less aroused than the low desire for control subjects before the procedure began. This finding indicates that high desire for control people do not typically operate at a higher arousal level than people with a low desire for control, but rather that they are more likely to react to certain events. When these high desire for control people have a history of heart problems, as did the subjects in the Hatton *et al.* study, the consequences for one's health can be serious.

In summary, although there is evidence that desire for control may be related to health, the exact nature of this relationship is far from clear. The few relevant studies we have suggest that high desire for control people approach health-related behaviors differently than people with a low desire for control. High desire for control people appear to engage in better health habits than low desire for control people, and it is quite probable that these good health habits eventually result in better health for these people than if they did not have these habits. However, high desire for control people may also be more prone to certain physiological reactions to stress that could have an adverse effect on their health, at least with certain types of patients.

SUMMARY

Who is more psychologically and physically healthy, high desire for control people or people with a low desire for control? The research reviewed in this chapter provides no simple answer to this question, probably because desire for control is linked to well-being and health in a number of complex ways. High desire for control people probably structure their lives to avoid stressful uncontrollable situations as much as possible. However, when problems develop, these people react differently than low desire for control people in a number of ways. Some research suggests that high desire for control people are more aroused physically than people with a low desire for control. People with a high desire for control may become more upset about a moderately stressful situation than low desire for control people, particularly if the situation is one that frustrates their need to feel in control. These people also are more likely to deal with the problem through active efforts to resolve the issue. High desire for control people are more likely than low desire for control people to try to deal with the situation themselves rather than rely on others or hope that things will work themselves out.

The results suggest that both a high desire for control and a low desire for control have their advantages. Low desire for control people, who are more likely to take things as they come, seem to have fewer stressful moments in their lives. However, perhaps because of their efficiency in dealing with problems, high desire for control people tend to look better on measures of anxiety and general well-being. Low desire for control people may be less susceptible to stress-induced health problems. However, the better health habits of high desire for control people probably help to keep them from suffering some preventable health problems.

A high desire for control might also be a cause as well as a symptom of psychological problems. Although high desire for control people typically deal with daily problems, they probably have a more difficult time than low desire for control people when facing a serious, uncontrollable problem. In addition, psychologists working with certain kinds of clients, such as adult children of alcoholics, have suggested that their clients' excessively high need for control is a symptom of larger psychological issues and a problem in dealing effectively with others.

Thus, the answer to the question about who is better off psychologically and physically probably depends on many factors. Research reviewed in other chapters indicates that a person's desire for control level affects many parts of his or her life, including achievement at work or school, interpersonal relations, and depression. All of these must be considered in determining a person's overall level of psychological health. What is clear is that a person's desire for control level plays an important role in his or her well-being, perhaps in many ways that have yet to be discovered.

CHAPTER 8

DEPRESSION

Research on the relationship between perceived control and depression has created a long and complex literature. For many years psychologists have observed that people suffering from depression felt they had little ability to control the events in their lives. It is not uncommon to hear a clinically depressed person say such things as "Nothing I do will make a difference," or "I can't change the way things are." Moreover, the passive behavior symptomatic of depression suggests that sufferers have little motivation to change their lives or make things better. This lack of motivation, a giving up in the face of problems or even when facing life's daily obstacles, is a primary characteristic of depression. In short, depressed people often appear to have very little desire to control the events in their lives.

DESIRE FOR CONTROL AND LEARNED HELPLESSNESS

Although it is clear that perceptions of and motivation for personal control are related to depression, teasing out the causal links in this relationship remains a challenge. However, for almost two decades an extensive amount of research has been devoted to this task. Most of this work has been stimulated by the theory of learned helplessness, which will be described briefly in the next section.

LEARNED HELPLESSNESS

In the mid 1970s, Martin Seligman and his colleagues proposed that depression sometimes results from learning that one is helpless to control important events (Seligman, 1975). In the original version of learned helplessness theory, depression was said to begin with the perception that some important event was outside one's control. For example, after repeated efforts to pass a difficult class or patch up a romantic relationship, a person might conclude that he or she is unable to control the situation. Such a response is probably correct and prudent in many situations. However, learned helplessness and the subsequent depression develop when this person then inappropriately generalizes this perception of no control to another situation over which some control is possible.

Thus, the woman who learns that she is helpless to avoid failing her math class may inappropriately perceive that she cannot control the outcome of other classes, whether or not she will get the job of her choice, if her relationships will work out, and so on. If unchecked, this inappropriate generalization will lead to a general approach to life typical of depressives who say "Nothing I do ever matters."

Early laboratory experiments with human subjects tended to support the original learned helplessness model (Hiroto, 1974; Hiroto & Seligman, 1975). In the typical research paradigm subjects were exposed to an aversive stimulus, such as a loud noise, that they either could or could not control, such as by solving a cognitive puzzle. After many trials, subjects in the learned helplessness condition came to accept that they could not control the aversive stimuli. These subjects then were taken out of the initial uncontrollable situation and presented with a task over which they had some control. As expected, the subjects who had experienced a lack of control during the helplessness training trials did worse on the posttraining task than subjects who either had been able to control the aversive stimuli or who had experienced no aversive stimuli. Researchers interpreted these findings to mean that the subjects had learned they were helpless in the initial situation and had inappropriately generalized that helplessness to the controllable situation. Although later findings would lead to modifications of the theory, considerable evidence was generated to support the idea that a perceived lack of control was often an important step in the development of depression.

IMPORTANCE OF CONTROL AND DEPRESSION

One of the key variables not specifically addressed in the original learned helplessness model is the extent to which the uncontrollable event is important to the individual. Obviously, there are many events in our daily lives that we simply do not care to control. These probably include what your spouse has for breakfast or what color shirt a co-worker wears. On the other hand, there are situations that nearly everyone is highly motivated to control to some extent, such as not being hit by a passing car or not losing one's job. However, there are a large number of events that fall somewhere in between these two extremes, and this is where individual differences come into play. For example, while one woman fumes in heavy traffic she cannot control, the man in the car next to her may simply take the inconvenience in stride. The difference between these two reactions to the same uncontrollable event may be the extent to which the woman and the man generally feel it is important to control the events in their lives, that is, their desire for control level.

Wortman and Brehm (1975) argued that the perceived importance of the event is a key variable in determining people's reaction to a lack of control. They proposed that people react to an uncontrollable situation with intense effort to exercise control when the event is relatively important to them. However, according to the model, if these people continue to find that their efforts to control the event are unproductive, they will eventually suffer from severe depression and learned helplessness. In the typical learned helplessness paradigm, these highly motivated people will try extra hard to solve the problems during the initial trials of the helplessness training. However, when they discover that the stimuli are uncontrollable, they should show greater learned helplessness on subsequent tasks than those who felt controlling the task was relatively unimportant to begin with.

What this line of reasoning suggests is that people who typically see control over events as important may be more susceptible to learned helplessness and depression than those who do not. In other words, because high desire for control people are more likely than low desire for control people to believe it is important to control a given event, they may be more susceptible to depression. As long as control is possible, high desire for control people can avoid learned helplessness. However, inevitably they will encounter situations they cannot control. In contrast, low desire for control people are less likely to react with either a great deal of effort or a great deal of depression when encountering an uncontrollable situation.

RESEARCH ON DESIRE FOR CONTROL
AND LEARNED HELPLESSNESS

Research examining the role desire for control plays in the development of learned helplessness attempts to answer two questions. First, are high desire for control people or low desire for control people more susceptible to depression in the typical learned helplessness situation?

The straightforward prediction from the reasoning described above is that high desire for control people should be more likely than people with a low desire for control to experience depression when they perceive a lack of personal control.

The second question is whether high desire for control people or low desire for control people suffer from depression more often and more severely. A case can be made for two opposing predictions. On the one hand, there are many uncontrollable events in our lives that both high desire for control people and low desire for control people are going to encounter. If high desire for control people are more likely than low desire for control people to respond to these inevitable experiences by becoming depressed, they may suffer from depression more frequently and perhaps more severely than people with a low desire for control.

However, one might also argue that high desire for control people have a couple of defenses that may keep them from being as vulnerable to depression as low desire for control people generally. First, because of their extra effort to exercise control, high desire for control people probably exert more control over the events in their lives than people with a low desire for control. Research demonstrating how high desire for control people try harder and achieve more than people with a low desire for control was reviewed in Chapter 5. Second, high desire for control people may be more likely than people with a low desire for control to perceive they have control over events when in fact they may not. Research indicating that high desire for control people sometimes maintain this inaccurate perception was reviewed in Chapter 6.

Thus, although we can predict that high desire for control people are more likely than low desire for control people to become depressed when facing uncontrollable stimuli like those used in learned helplessness experiments, it is not clear that they are necessarily more susceptible to depression in their everyday lives. My colleagues and I have conducted a series of studies designed to test these hypotheses.

We first examined the relationship between desire for control and depression by adapting the basic learned helplessness laboratory paradigm (Burger & Arkin, 1980). The primary purpose of this study was to separate the effects of controllability and predictability that had been confounded in earlier learned helplessness research. Helplessness was induced through fifty 20-second trials in which subjects tried to turn off an aversive noise by solving an anagram problem. As in the traditional paradigm, sometimes the anagrams were solvable, thus allowing subjects to exercise control over the noise, and sometimes no control was possible. In addition, sometimes the influence over the noise occurred in a predictable manner and other times it was not predictable. A comparison group did not go through the helplessness-training trials. We measured depression with an adjective checklist before and after the trials, and also examined cognitive performance with a memory task.

The results suggested that controllability and predictability may both play a role in the development of learned helplessness. When subjects received either controllable or predictable aversive noise they were no different on performance or affect measures than the no-noise comparison group. However, a secondary concern in this experiment was to examine the role of individual differences in desire for control. We divided subjects into halves based on desire for control within each condition. The results from the memory task, collapsed across the predictability–unpredictability variable, are presented in Table 8-1. As seen in the table, high desire for control subjects and low desire for control subjects in the no-noise comparison group performed nearly identically on the memory task. However, the high desire for control subjects appeared to have a stronger reaction to the noise experience generally than did the low desire for control subjects. The strongest evidence of learned helplessness was found among the high desire for control subjects who were exposed to the uncontrollable noise, although the interaction effect for this analysis fell short of statistical significance.

The results from the affect data were less clear. To aid in interpreting these data, the mean posttraining depression scores are included in Table 8-2 for all 10 conditions. Most notable in these data is that high desire for control subjects generally report higher levels of depression than subjects with a low desire for control. When the pretraining depression scores were used as a covariate, a significant main effect was found for desire for control.

Thus, the findings from the Burger and Arkin (1980) experiment provide some support for the hypothesis that high desire for control people are more susceptible to depression than people with a low desire for control when encountering uncontrollable events. The experiment also uncovered data consistent with the notion that high desire for control people experience depression more often and more severely than

TABLE 8-1. Mean Number of Errors on Memory Task

	High desire for control	Low desire for control
Controllable noise	33.5	30.0
Uncontrollable noise	35.7	33.6
No noise	31.4	31.2

Note: From Burger and Arkin (1980); copyright © 1980 by the American Psychological Association; reprinted by permission of the publisher

TABLE 8-2. Mean Posttraining Depression Scores

	High desire for control		Low desire for control	
	Controllable	Uncontrollable	Controllable	Uncontrollable
Predictable	16.9	15.2	14.0	14.9
Unpredictable	16.6	18.0	13.9	17.7
No-noise	13.0		9.6	

Note: From Burger and Arkin (1980); copyright © 1980 by the American Psychological Association; reprinted by permission of the publisher

people with a low desire for control generally. The largest difference between high desire for control subjects and low desire for control subjects was found in the no-noise comparison group. This finding suggests that the high desire for control subjects showed up for the experiment with higher levels of depression than the low desire for control subjects. Of course, it is also possible that merely participating in the rather non-threatening comparison group procedures resulted in an increase in negative mood for these high desire for control subjects.

A subsequent study examined more specifically the role that a lack of perceived control plays in the development of depression among people with a high desire for control. I asked people in this unpublished study to describe why they thought they had become depressed during a recent experience with depression. I expected that high desire for control people would be more likely than people with a low desire for control to identify a lack of control as a reason for their depression. I made this prediction for two reasons. First, because control is more important for high desire for control people, they should be more susceptible than low desire for control people to becoming depressed over uncontrollable events. Second, high desire for control people are generally more aware of their ability to control or not control events than are people with a low desire for control. This attention to the issue of controllability might also lead high desire for control people to more often identify a lack of control as part of a situation they find depressing.

I asked 69 undergraduates to think about a depressing experience they had gone through during the past six months. Subjects read on a confidential and anonymous questionnaire that this experience could be something that had only left them feeling a little sad to something that was painfully depressing. The questionnaire emphasized that subjects were free to select any experience that they would be willing to answer some questions about, and that they could choose to not answer this part of the questionnaire or stop at any time. The questions about depression came at the end of a questionnaire that contained several inventories, including the DC Scale.

After identifying a depressing experience, subjects were asked to rate on a nine-point scale how depressed they had become during the most severe part of the experience. They were then asked, "Why do you think you became depressed?" Subjects were given about half a page to answer this question. Because I was looking to see if subjects would spontaneously identify a lack of control as a cause of their depression, I chose to ask an open-ended question in this way rather than provide any priming cues about control or related issues in the question. Thus, it was after this open-ended question that the questionnaire ended with a traditional Likert-type question asking specifically about control. Subjects were asked to rate on an 11-point scale how much control they thought they had over the event that led to the depression.

I found no relationship whatsoever between desire for control level and the severity of the depressing experience subjects chose to write about, as shown in Table 8-3. However, the primary purpose of the study was to determine if subjects would spontaneously identify a lack of control over the event as a reason for why they became depressed. To examine this, two judges independently coded responses to the open-ended item for the number of references subjects made to being unable to control the event. Statements such as "Could not do anything about," "Felt helpless," "Could not stop," and "Could not influence" were counted. As shown in Table 8-3, a significant correlation was found between desire for control scores and the number of such statements subjects included in their responses. The higher their desire for control score, the more often subjects made references to a lack of control as a cause of their depression. A similar correlation was found between desire for control and subjects' responses to the Likert-type item. The higher the desire for control score, the less control subjects reported feeling over the depressing event.

In summary, the findings from both of these studies support the hypothesis that high desire for control people are more susceptible to depression when they experience uncontrollable events. However, whether this means that high desire for control people suffer from depression

TABLE 8-3. Correlations between DC Scale and Dependent Measures

	Correlation with DC Scale	p value
Severity of depressing event	.00	ns
Number of statements indicating a lack of control	.25	$p < .05$
Perceived control over event (Likert-type item)	.20	$p < .07$

more than people with a low desire for control generally remains unclear from these data. Although high desire for control people and low desire for control people did not differ in the severity they reported for their experience with depression in the second study, this item is a poor indicator of depression level. What is needed is a more direct assessment of depression. This was done in the research reported in the next section.

INTERACTION WITH LOCUS OF CONTROL

As described in Chapter 2, a great deal of research over the past few decades has been concerned with individual differences in locus of control. In contrast to desire for control, which is concerned with how much control people want, locus of control refers to how much control people believe they typically have over events. Scores on measures of the two constructs are sometimes slightly correlated, depending upon which locus of control scale researchers use. However, it is possible to identify people who, for example, have a high desire for control but an external locus of control.

At the risk of sounding overly simplistic, I have found it useful to divide people into four categories depending upon how they score on measures of desire for control and locus of control, as shown in Table 8-4. What kind of characteristics might we find in people falling into each of the four groups? High desire for control people who also see themselves as largely responsible for the events in their lives probably would be relatively productive and content. Low desire for control people who generally hold an external locus of control might not be as productive, but would probably also be relatively content, if not typically less stressed. It is interesting to speculate about the low desire for control people who also have an internal locus of control. Although I have no data on this question, I could guess that these people suffer from anxiety

TABLE 8-4. Model for
Desire for Control and Locus of Control

		Desire for Control	
		High	Low
Locus of Control	Internal	Achieving	Anxious
	External	Depressed	Content

more frequently than most. In essence, people falling into this category do not want much control, but feel they have more than they can handle.

But the most interesting category for the discussion here concerns those people with a high desire for control and an external locus of control. In a sense, these people approach life in a manner that resembles the typical learned helplessness laboratory procedure. It is important for them to control many of the situations they encounter, but they also tend to believe they are unable to exert much influence over these situations. This sounds like a prescription for learned helplessness and depression. Thus, it may be that this subset of high desire for control people are the ones who are most prone to bouts of depression.

I tested this hypothesis in two longitudinal studies. The first study looked at how desire for control and locus of control were related to depression over a six-month period (Burger, 1984). Undergraduates participated in the experiment during the first month of the school year, and again six months later. During the initial contact subjects completed the Beck Depression Inventory (Beck, 1972), the Levenson Locus of Control Scales (Levenson, 1981), and the DC Scale. As described in Chapter 2, the Levenson scales divide locus of control beliefs into three categories: Internal, Powerful Others, and Chance. The second phase of the study was carried out through a mail survey questionnaire, returned by 71 of the 99 students who participated in the initial data collection. The second questionnaire asked subjects about their experiences with depression during the previous six months. This questionnaire included the Beck Depression Inventory modified to gauge subjects' experiences with depression since the beginning of the school year (instead of at that moment).

The design allowed me to look at how the desire for control and locus of control were related to depression scores at the time the inventories were completed and how well the scales could predict experiences with depression over the following six months. The initial analysis found only a moderate correlation between desire for control and Beck Depression Inventory scores at the time of the testing $(r = -.23)$. Given all of the many variables that contribute to depression, it is perhaps not surprising that the correlation was not larger. The correlation might also have been restricted by the narrow range of scores found when administering the Beck Scale to relatively nondepressed college students. However, I was surprised to find that the correlation was in the opposite direction of what I had expected. That is, lower desire for control scores were associated with higher levels of depression, albeit slightly short of statistical significance. The correlation between desire for control and the Beck Scale taken six months later was even lower $(r = -.14)$.

Several significant findings emerged in a series of regression analyses conducted to look at the interaction between desire for control and each of the three locus of control scales. Most of these findings revealed significant relationships among the locus of control scores and various measures of depression, consistent with earlier research. However, there also were two interesting sets of interactions between locus of control and desire for control. First, high desire for control people reported seeking out help from a friend or relative for a problem they found depressing more often than people with a low desire for control. As shown in Table 8-5, this effect reflects an interaction with locus of control. High desire for control subjects who also scored low on the Internal Scale, high on the Powerful Others Scale, and high on the Chance Scale reported seeking help from nonprofessionals more often than subjects in any of the other conditions. In other words, people with a high need for control who also generally believe that solutions to problems are outside of their control were most likely to seek out someone who could help them deal with their problem.

This same pattern was found for an item asking subjects if they had ever thought about the possibility of committing suicide during the previous six months. As shown in Table 8-6, significant interactions were found between desire for control and two of the locus of control scales when comparing subjects who reported having such thoughts at least once with those who reported no suicidal thoughts during this time. Suicidal thoughts were highest among those who had a high desire for control but who also reported that they typically felt they had little control over events.

Thus, the findings provide some support for the prediction that desire for control interacts with locus of control to affect depression. When significant interactions were found, subjects with a high desire for control were the most likely to report depression. These findings are

TABLE 8-5. Mean Number of Times Subjects Sought Help
from a Friend or Relative for a Problem They Found Depressing

	High desire for control	Low desire for control
High internal	2.45	5.50
Low internal	15.00	2.78
High powerful others	12.50	2.75
Low powerful others	1.19	4.41
High chance	14.44	3.35
Low chance	2.05	3.88

Note: From Burger (1984); reprinted by permission

TABLE 8-6. Percentage of Subjects Reporting
Suicidal Thoughts at Least Once During Six-Month Period

	High desire for control	Low desire for control
High internal	20.0	0
Low internal	22.2	24.0
High chance	50.0	25.0
Low chance	8.3	5.9

Note: From Burger (1984); reprinted by permission

particularly impressive given that the depression measures were taken
six months after the individual difference variables were measured. However, as in the earlier research, there was no suggestion that a high desire
for control necessarily leads to more frequent or more severe experiences
with depression. If anything, the data in the Burger (1984) study found
a slight tendency for low desire for control people to be more depressed
than people with a high desire for control.

Before interpreting the results of the Burger (1984) investigation, let
us look at a replication of this study that included some important proce-
dural changes. Crowe and Burger (1984) used procedures similar to those
in the earlier study, with the following improvements. First, depression
levels were measured at the time desire for control and locus of control
were measured, and again at one-month and then six-month intervals.
Second, we asked subjects to report on their depression for the past week,
rather than asking them to reflect on the past six months, as in the earlier
study. Third, we used the Center for Epidemiologic Studies–Depression
Scale (CES-D Scale) (Radloff, 1977) to measure depression. The CES-D
Scale is more appropriate for a college student population and provides
a wider range of scores than the Beck Scale used in the Burger (1984)
study. In addition, we simplified the analyses by only administering the
Chance Scale, which had been the best predictor in the initial study.

As shown in Table 8-7, the DC Score did not correlate with depression level at any of the three testing times nor with an overall depression

TABLE 8-7. Correlations between
Desire for Control, Chance, and Depression Scores

	Initial testing	One-month follow-up	Six-month follow-up	Overall score
DC Scale	−.02	.00	−.13	−.06
Chance Scale	.33**	.27*	.16	.31*

Note: * $p < .05$; ** $p < .01$; from Crowe and Burger (1984)

score created from aggregating the three CES-D scores. As in the earlier study, a higher belief that one's life is controlled by chance was related to higher levels of depression. Interestingly, desire for control and chance scores were not correlated in this study, $r = -.04$.

We found a significant interaction between desire for control and chance on the initial and overall depression scores. As shown in Table 8-8, we found the same pattern in the one-month and six-month follow-up measures, but these effects fell just short of statistical significance. However, the pattern shown in the table was not quite the same one uncovered in the Burger (1984) study. As in the earlier study, high desire for control subjects who also held a strong belief that chance controlled the events in their lives tended to have the highest depression scores. However, the interaction is caused largely by the high desire for control subjects who held a low belief in chance.

How can we explain this last finding? The interaction suggests that people who typically want to control the events in their lives and who believe that this need is met most of the time are less likely to experience depression than those who either have a low need for control or who typically perceive that they do not have control. That externals typically have higher depression levels than internals is consistent with research on the relationship between locus of control and depression. In a meta-analysis of ninety-seven studies, Benassi, Sweeney, and Dufour (1988) found an average correlation of .31 between measures of locus of control and depression, indicating that an external locus of control is associated with more depression. But why would internals with a high desire for control have lower depression scores than internals with a low desire for control? No clear answers emerge from examining the data from either the Burger (1984) or Crowe and Burger (1984) studies.

However, the findings from both studies do suggest that the link between depression and desire for control alone is at best a weak one. I have found no evidence for the expectation that high desire for control people would suffer from depression more often and more severely than

TABLE 8-8. Mean Depression Scores

| | High desire for control | | Low desire for control | |
	High chance	Low chance	High chance	Low chance
Initial testing	17.50	6.92	15.12	12.25
One-month follow-up	13.00	7.23	12.50	13.88
Six-month follow-up	10.56	5.54	13.06	11.75
Overall score	13.69	6.56	13.56	12.62

Note: From Crowe and Burger (1984)

people with a low desire for control. However, some high desire for control people may be more or less vulnerable to depression than others, depending upon their locus of control level. Unfortunately, exactly what this relationship is remains unclear at the present time.

ATTRIBUTIONS AND ATTRIBUTIONAL STYLE

By the late 1970s it was becoming clear to researchers that there were many limitations and exceptions to the original learned helplessness model. Many investigations failed to support predictions derived from the theory, and still others found results in the opposite direction of what the theory would lead them to expect (cf. Costello, 1978; Roth, 1980). Consequently, the original learned helplessness model was modified to include a consideration of how people explain the reasons for their lack of control (Abramson, Seligman, & Teasdale, 1978; Miller & Norman, 1979).

According to the reformulated theory, learned helplessness begins when a person experiences an important uncontrollable event, probably one with negative consequences. At this point people ask themselves why they cannot control the event. Depending upon the answer, they may or may not become depressed. Abramson *et al.* (1978) proposed that these attributions can be examined along three dimensions. People are most likely to become depressed when they explain their lack of control in terms of internal, stable and global causes. That is, depression results from attributing the lack of control to something about yourself, something that will not go away anytime soon, and something that applies to many other situations.

In yet another elaboration of the learned helplessness model, Seligman and his colleagues proposed that some people have a relatively stable attributional style that may make them prone to making the kinds of attributions that lead to frequent experiences with depression (Peterson, Semmel, von Baeyer, Abramson, Metalsky, & Seligman, 1982). That is, some people have a tendency to explain uncontrollable events in terms of internal, stable, and global attributions. Consequently, these people are more prone to suffering from depression. Some research supports this notion, but reviews suggest that this support is far from conclusive (Peterson, Villanova, & Raps, 1985; Robins, 1988).

Is desire for control related to attributional style? Peterson *et al.* (1982) developed the Attribution Style Questionnaire (ASQ) to measure the extent to which people typically rely on internal, stable, and global attributions. The scale also measures the importance people typically

TABLE 8-9. Correlations between
DC Scale and Attribution Style Questionnaire Subscales

Subscale	Positive events	Negative events
Internality	.13	−.11
Stability	.22*	−.02
Globality	.22*	−.08
Importance	.18	.02

Note: *p < .10; from Burger (1985); copyright © 1985 by the American
Psychological Association; reprinted by permission of the publisher

place on the outcome of events. I gave the ASQ and the DC Scale to a group of undergraduates (Burger, 1985). However, as seen in Table 8-9, the correlations tended to be low and nonsignificant. Moreover, the direction of the correlations argues, if anything, that high desire for control people should be less susceptible to depression. These subjects tended to make internal, stable, and global attributions for successes, and showed the opposite pattern for failures.

The pattern of correlations also is consistent with the research presented in Chapter 5 demonstrating that high desire for control people make the kinds of attributions that are associated with success and achievement, not depression. I should also note that one reason for the low correlations between desire for control and attributional style may have to do with the relatively poor reliability of the ASQ scales. As Peterson et al. (1982) report, the subscales have internal consistencies that make finding significant correlations with other measures difficult. Nonetheless, whatever the relationship between desire for control and depression, it does not appear to be a function of the types of attributions high desire for control people make for their successes and failures.

SUMMARY

Although the research reviewed in this chapter indicates that desire for control is related to depression, the nature of that relationship remains rather fuzzy at this time. Some evidence indicates that encountering important uncontrollable events is more likely to trigger depression in high desire for control people than in people with a low desire for control. However, this does not mean that high desire for control people are generally more likely than low desire for control people to become depressed. Correlations between desire for control and measures of depression are modest at best, and the results of one study suggested that low desire for control people may be more depressed than people with a high desire for control.

This latter finding makes sense if we look at the causal link between desire for control and depression from a different perspective. That is, a low desire for control may be caused by the depression, rather than the other way around. We know that depressed people often express limited efforts to change their circumstances. Thus, if we measure depression and desire for control at the same time, we should not be surprised to find some evidence for a low desire for control among depressed people.

In contrast to this explanation, the findings from the Burger (1984) study indicated that high desire for control people are more likely than low desire for control people to show certain signs of depression, but only when they also have an external locus of control. However, a closer examination of the data suggests yet another possibility. It may be that the high desire for control people did not suffer more depression, but rather that they dealt with their depression differently. That is, externals with a high desire for control were more likely than other subjects to seek help for their problem from a friend or relative. For someone who wants to do something about the depression and who typically sees control over events in the hands of others, seeking help from someone else makes good sense.

In short, the research reported here only begins to untie the ways desire for control is related to depression. The only consistent finding seems to be that a lack of control is more likely to lead to depression among high desire for control people than people with a low desire for control. Prospective studies with populations other than undergraduates certainly are needed. While the research conducted thus far hints that desire for control may play a role in the development of depression, it also suggests that the relationship may be a complex one involving other variables and one that, for the moment, remains somewhat elusive.

GAMBLING BEHAVIOR

People who never gamble or who limit themselves to an occasional football bet or lottery ticket have a difficult time understanding the millions of Americans who bet and inevitably lose large amounts of money they often cannot afford. Common sense should tell us that casinos are not built by giving away money and that the more people play at games of chance the less likely they are to come out ahead. Yet Americans continue to spend billions of dollars each year gambling. Although the numbers are difficult to estimate, there may be hundreds of thousands of Americans with compulsive gambling problems.

Certainly there are many variables that contribute to problem gambling. However, how people play games of *chance* is particularly interesting from a perceived control perspective. By definition, games such as craps, roulette, lotteries, slot machines, bingo, and so on are determined by chance. That is, there is no logical way the player can influence the outcome of the game. In addition, the odds for these games are set in favor of the house. This means that a player cannot come out ahead without relying on some good luck. Luck, of course, is something the player has no control over. Nonetheless, millions of people invest large amounts of money into this uncontrollable activity.

How do individual differences in desire for control relate to gambling behavior? At first glance, we might think that high desire for control people would shun gambling. Why would they have any interest in risking their money on something that they obviously cannot control? However, a closer examination of how high desire for control people and low desire for control people process information about their ability to control events (see Chapter 6) suggests another possibility. Although high desire for control people dislike situations they are unable to control, the amount of control they believe they have over a given outcome may not always be accurate. As described in the next section, their high need to control events may make high desire for control people more vulnerable to illusions of control than people with a low desire for control.

THE ILLUSION OF CONTROL

Several investigations have demonstrated that under certain conditions people typically come to believe they have some control over events that are otherwise obviously determined by chance (Langer, 1975; Langer & Roth, 1975; Strickland, Lewicki & Katz, 1966; Wortman, 1975). The illusion of control is best illustrated in games of chance, and is most likely to be found in situations resembling those where the outcome can be influenced by ability or effort. For example, subjects have been found to make larger bets, an indication of their perceived control, when they are told ahead of time what number they are shooting for in a dice game, even though players have no ability to control the outcome of the toss (Strickland *et al.*, 1966). Subjects in another study were more confident that their lottery ticket would be the winner when they chose the ticket themselves than when simply given a ticket by the seller (Langer, 1975). Although the odds of winning are no different in either situation, subjects apparently felt they somehow had the ability to select the winning ticket when given the opportunity.

Many gambling games are set up to foster this illusion of control. You might see a demonstration of this effect when watching people play slot machines. Many players have special ways of pulling the handle, depositing the money, or watching as the pictures come up. Some seem to think that pulling hard and then letting go will do it. Others believe that closing one eye, pulling with their left hand, crossing themselves, or not looking until they hear the coins dropping into their tray is the way to increase their chances of success. How much control would people feel over a machine that took their money and then simply told them whether or not they had won? Even if the odds of winning were the same with this machine as with the typical slot machine, I suspect that players would be less interested in the machine they obviously could not influence. After all, with such a machine winning and losing would just be a matter of chance!

How is desire for control related to the illusion of control? Research reviewed in Chapter 6 demonstrates that high desire for control people are more likely than low desire for control people to interpret their own behavior in terms of control. When they won at the beginning of a sequence of coin tosses, high desire for control subjects tended to believe they would be able to guess correctly nearly 60% of the time on an upcoming series of coin tosses (Burger, 1986). In contrast, low desire for control subjects were relatively accurate in their estimates. This finding suggests that high desire for control people may be more susceptible to the illusion of control than people with a low desire for control. Not only are high desire for control people more likely to attend to cues indicating that they can control the event, they also are so motivated to see themselves in control that they may distort their perception of control to satisfy that need.

This reasoning leads to another interesting possibility. If high desire for control people are more susceptible to the illusion of control, and if many gambling games are set up to provide an illusion of control, high desire for control people may be more vulnerable to problem gambling than people with a low desire for control. I have begun to examine this possibility in research reviewed later in this chapter. However, first it is necessary to test the first part of this hypothesis, that high desire for control people are more susceptible than low desire for control people to the illusion of control. This prediction was examined in a series of laboratory experiments.

LABORATORY INVESTIGATIONS ON THE ILLUSION OF CONTROL

I looked at the desire for control–illusion of control relationship in the first experiment ever conducted with the Desirability of Control Scale (Burger & Cooper, 1979). Undergraduates signed up for what they believed to be an experiment on gambling behavior. They were given 50 poker chips, told to refer to them as dollars, and asked to play the game as if playing with $50 of their own money. The game consisted of betting on whether a pair of rolled dice would add up to the target number on each of 18 games. The experimenter explained that the target number would change for each game, but that the payoff would change accordingly. For example, if the target number were 9, then subjects would be paid off in a 9:1 ratio, because that is how frequently the number would appear by chance. The experimenter continued the explanation until it was clear the subject understood the payoff ratio system.

Subjects also were randomly assigned to either a bet-before or bet-after condition. The bet-before condition was designed to create an illusion of control. Subjects in this condition were told before they threw the dice what the target number was and were asked how many chips they wanted to bet that they would throw the number on the next dice toss (up to a limit of five chips per game). In other words, these subjects knew what number they were trying to throw. Subjects in the bet-after condition were instructed to toss the dice first, but to keep them hidden under a cup. Then they were told what the target number was and asked how much they wanted to bet. The chances of winning were identical in both conditions, but in the latter condition the subjects did not know what number they hoped to throw when tossing the dice.

The total number of chips bet over the 18 games was used as the measure of illusion of control. As shown in Table 9-1, the high desire for control subjects in the bet-before condition bet significantly more chips than did subjects in any of the other conditions. Subjects with a low desire for control did not alter their bets as a function of which condition they were in. In other words, although a strong illusion of control was found for the high desire for control subjects, no effect was found for the low desire for control subjects.

Other laboratory investigations have replicated and extended this basic effect, but sometimes under limited conditions. For example, in one study subjects were given 50 poker chips to bet with during 14 card games (Burger & Schnerring, 1982). In the condition designed to create an illusion of control, subjects shuffled the kings and queens from a deck of playing cards and placed the eight cards face down on a table. They were then told what the target suit was and asked how much they would bet that they could select either the king or queen from that suit with one guess. Again, the experimenter explained why the payoff ratio was set at 3:1 for each game until the subject appeared to understand the concept. A similar procedure was used in another condition, except the experimenter shuffled the cards, placed them on the table, and the experimenter selected one of the cards. Subjects in this condition also were asked to place their bets as to whether or not the card selected (but not turned over) by the experimenter would match the target suit that the experimenter would name after the bet. Thus, although many aspects of the situation differed, the chances of winning were the same in both conditions.

We also added another variable to this design. Half the subjects were

TABLE 9-1. Mean Total Number of Chips Bet

	High desire for control	Low desire for control
Bet before condition	37.2	22.8
Bet after condition	25.3	20.9

Note: From Burger and Cooper (1979); reprinted by permission

told they could exchange the chips they had left at the end of the 14 trials for prizes. The prizes ranged from T-shirts to chewing gum, depending upon how many chips subjects had left. The other half heard nothing about prizes and were told to play the experiment like a game.

The results tended to replicate those in the earlier experiment. As shown in Table 9-2, high desire for control subjects bet the most when they were in the illusion of control condition. However, this effect was found only among the subjects who were playing for prizes. When subjects approached the task as a game, no differences were found for high desire for control subjects or low desire for control subjects in either condition.

The results of this experiment lead to a couple of interesting suggestions. First, it may be that high desire for control people do not always fall for the illusion of control, but rather only when it is relatively important for them to be able to control the situation, such as when prizes are at stake. This would mean that the subjects in the earlier experiment who were asked to play with the poker chips as if they were real dollars followed our instructions well. Second, the findings hint that desire for control might be applicable to real gambling situations. Although the stakes were relatively trivial in our experiment, high desire for control subjects were more likely than low desire for control subjects to succumb to the illusion of control in this gambling game when something of monetary value was at stake. Although we made it clear to subjects at the beginning of the experiment that even small prizes could be obtained with a final total of 50 chips (the amount they started with), some subjects could not resist risking these prizes in the hope of winning larger ones.

Other researchers have examined the relationship between desire for control and the illusion of control effect using a variation of the bet-before bet-after procedure from the Burger and Cooper (1979) experiment. For example, Wolfgang and Zenker (1982) failed to produce a basic illusion of control effect with their procedures, but nonetheless found a significant main effect for the desire for control variable. High desire for control subjects bet more than low desire for control subjects

TABLE 9-2. Mean Total Number of Chips Bet

	Reward		No reward	
	High desire for control	Low desire for control	High desire for control	Low desire for control
Illusion of control condition	46.45	34.75	39.25	41.50
No illusion of control condition	35.90	40.62	38.50	42.75

Note: From Burger and Schnerring (1982); reprinted by permission

across all conditions. Wolfgang, Zenker, and Viscusi (1984) examined the impact of long versus short odds within this paradigm. Subjects bet when the odds of winning were either 2:1, 7:1, or 18:1. The high desire for control subjects in this study bet more than the subjects with a low desire for control, but only when the odds were a rather conservative 2:1. As in the Burger and Cooper (1979) study, subjects in both of these experiments played with poker chips and were told only to act as if they were playing with real dollars.

This latter finding is a particularly interesting one. It seems as if the high desire for control subjects in this experiment were unable to risk their money when the chances of winning were fairly unlikely. However, these subjects were more likely to take the risk when they had a relatively high probability of winning. Nonetheless, because the payoffs were adjusted according to the odds, this finding again represents a type of illusion of control. That is, betting and winning at the rate expected by chance would result in the same amount of money over a large number of trials for someone betting on the high-payoff 18:1 long–shot as for someone betting on the small-payoff 2:1 odds. Unlike the low desire for control subjects, the subjects with a high desire for control appeared to have succumbed to the illusion that somehow they were capable of beating the game that otherwise was obviously determined by chance.

Data from an unpublished master's thesis by Hayes (1988) also provide a demonstration of this effect. Hayes modified the earlier Burger and Cooper (1979) bet-before bet-after procedure by offering subjects prizes for winning. He also selected subjects from extreme ends of the distribution from both the DC Scale and Zuckerman's (1979) Sensation Seeking Scale. Although this unique sample makes direct comparisons with the other studies difficult, the findings are consistent with those from the earlier investigations. Hayes found significantly higher rates of betting only for subjects who were considerably above the mean in both desire for control and sensation seeking.

Another experiment demonstrating the tendency for high desire for control people to succumb to the illusion of control more readily than low desire for control people looked at the effects of playing with familiar versus unfamiliar materials. Langer (1975) found that people had more confidence in their lottery ticket when it contained a familiar letter of the alphabet than when it contained an unusual symbol. She reasoned that it is more difficult to control something that is unfamiliar. Thus it is more difficult for people to develop an illusion of control when they are dealing with unfamiliar materials.

Based on this reasoning, I expected that the tendency for high desire for control people to succumb to the illusion of control would be weakened when playing with unfamiliar materials. To test this prediction, I had undergraduates play twelve trials of a card selection game (Burger, 1986). As in some of the earlier studies, subjects understood that they could trade in their poker chips at the end of the game for prizes. Each trial of the game consisted of subjects shuffling four cards and then laying the cards face down on a table. For half the subjects the cards consisted of the four aces from a deck of playing cards. Other subjects played with four cards containing unusual symbols created for the experiment. The experimenter indicated the winning card for each trial by selecting a card from an identical deck. Subjects then bet on their likelihood of selecting the same card from the four laid out before them. The results mirrored the earlier findings. High desire for control subjects bet significantly more than subjects with a low desire for control, but this effect was enhanced when they played with the familiar cards instead of the ones with the unfamiliar symbols.

One final laboratory experiment should be mentioned here. As described in Chapter 6, we asked subjects to guess the outcome of 30 coin tosses (Burger, 1986). Although all subjects received feedback indicating they had guessed correctly on 15 out of 30 trials, high desire for control subjects who believed they had guessed well at the beginning of the sequence were more likely than low desire for control subjects to attribute their performance to ability and to estimate that they would do better than chance on 100 more trials. Although subjects were not playing for prizes, these high desire for control subjects clearly were demonstrating an illusion of control over an event otherwise obviously determined by chance.

In summary, a large number of laboratory investigations have been conducted comparing reactions to simulated gambling situations of high desire for control subjects and low desire for control subjects. The overall pattern that emerges from this work is that high desire for control people are more likely than low desire for control people to express an illusion that they are able to control the outcome of events determined by chance. This illusion of control can be created through a number of different procedures, such as being able to throw the dice, playing with familiar materials, or winning toward the beginning of a sequence of games. Other research indicates that this effect can also be influenced by a number of variables, such as long versus short odds, sensation-seeking level, and whether the subject is playing for tangible rewards. Nonetheless, when differences are found, it has always been the high desire for control subjects who have demonstrated the greatest illusion of control. I must point out, however, that there is a degree of irony in this. By succumbing to the illusion of control, high desire for control people are, in effect, engaging in just the kind of behavior they prefer to avoid.

DESIRE FOR CONTROL
AND REAL-WORLD GAMBLING BEHAVIOR

It is extremely tempting to interpret the results from the laboratory experiments described above to suggest that individual differences in desire for control play a role in real gambling behavior. More intriguing yet is the possibility that individual differences in desire for control may play a role in the etiology of problem gambling. If, as suggested in the laboratory experiments, high desire for control people are more susceptible to believing they can control games of chance, then directions for treating problem gamblers might also be suggested.

However, making the leap from laboratory settings to real-world problems is always risky, and that may be particularly true in this case. We should keep in mind that none of the laboratory procedures dealt with real gambling, although a few began to resemble gambling with the offer of prizes. To my knowledge, none of the subjects in these experiments had a problem with gambling or even gambled occasionally, although it is most likely that a few did. The laboratory subjects also had little choice but to participate in the gambling-type games. This limitation prevents us from examining one of the most important steps in a real gambling situation, namely the individual's decision to seek out and engage in this behavior.

DESIRE FOR CONTROL AND PROBLEM GAMBLING

Nonetheless, the findings from the laboratory studies are suggestive. They indicate that high desire for control people may be more susceptible to problem gambling than people with a low desire for control. These laboratory results suggest that high desire for control people are more susceptible to the illusion of control, to believing that somehow they are going to be the one who beats the odds and wins big at the racetrack or in the casino. As shown in the Burger and Schnerring (1982) experiment, high desire for control people seem to be especially susceptible to this illusion of control when the stakes are real. Although small prizes were used in that study, we can imagine how important winning would be when dealing with thousands and perhaps, in the case of state lotteries today, millions of dollars.

Further, the coin-toss experiment suggests that high desire for control people are more susceptible to an illusion of control if they win during their first few experiences with the game. Thus, high desire for control people who have a good day at the racetrack the first few times they try betting on the horses may come to believe that somehow they have the ability to pick winners. Extended losing streaks, along with extensive monetary losses, may not easily convince these high desire for control people that their initial winnings were the result of luck and that they are unable to beat the odds after all. Taken together, the laboratory findings certainly make a case to hypothesize that desire for control plays a role in real-world gambling.

Although the number of studies examining desire for control and gambling behavior outside of the laboratory is limited at this time, I have data that shed some light on this relationship. Two separate questions are addressed in these data. First, does a person's desire for control level influence *how* he or she gambles? Second, does a person's desire for control level influence *if* and *how much* he or she gambles? Although we are far from any definitive answers to either of these questions, the results do provide some insights.

Research with Real Gamblers

The first study to examine the relationship between desire for control and gambling behavior in real gamblers looked at members of a local Gamblers Anonymous chapter (Burger & Smith, 1985). There are, of course, advantages and disadvantages to studying this group. On the positive side, these gamblers identified themselves for us as problem gamblers, and were likely to be honest in discussing their habits and losses. On the negative side, we cannot know how representative this group of men and women is of gamblers or even problem gamblers in general. Gamblers Anonymous members typically have hit bottom with their habit and have taken positive steps to get their lives back in order. Nonetheless, these former gamblers provided us with information about their serious gambling problems.

Subjects completed a short questionnaire asking about some demographic information, their approximate annual income when they were gambling, and how much money they lost in their worst year of gambling. In addition, subjects rated on five-point scales how frequently they had bet on poker and card games, horse racing, casino games, sports events, and lotteries. They also completed the Desirability of Control Scale.

Two other groups of subjects were used to help us interpret the data from the Gamblers Anonymous members. First, we located a matched control group of men and women who did not have a gambling problem.

Next, we asked undergraduates to rate on nine-point scales the extent to which they felt a bettor could have an influence over winning and losing on each of the five gambling situations we had asked the gamblers about. We collected these latter data to help us demonstrate that some gambling events provide more of an illusion of control than others. The results, shown in Table 9-3, were as expected. The subjects believed that bettors had some control over whether or not they won at card games, horse race betting, and sports event betting, but almost no control over casino games and lotteries.

The first question is whether the level of desire for control influenced how the Gamblers Anonymous members played when they had gambled. The answer appears to be that it did. We looked at how often the gamblers reported playing the three illusion-of-control games identified by our undergraduates: poker and card games, horse racing, and sports events. In truth, there is a small element of skill in playing poker, picking winning horses, and selecting winning football teams. However, it is precisely this small element of control that may make people betting on these events particularly vulnerable to believing they can exert enough control to win large amounts of money. In other words, these situations all contain a small element of an illusion of control.

Consequently, we calculated how often the gamblers reported having played the three illusion-of-control games. This score correlated significantly with their desire for control scores, $r = .46$. However, desire for control did not correlate with how frequently they had played the two low-illusion games, $r = .04$. In other words, the higher the desire for control, the more likely subjects were to have bet on the event, but only if the event contained an element of the illusion of control. In this way the high desire for control gamblers were very much like the high desire for control subjects in the laboratory experiments who increased

TABLE 9-3. Mean Rating of Chance
versus Skill Influence on Gambling Games

	Mean rating
Sports events	5.98
Poker and card games	5.42
Horse racing	4.83
Casino games (craps, roulette, slot machines)	2.11
Lotteries	1.62

Note: Subjects rated each item on a scale with 1 = completely chance and 9 = completely skill; from Burger and Smith (1985); copyright © The Society for Personality and Social Psychology; reprinted by permission of Sage Publications

their bets only when the situation hinted at an illusion of control. Thus, desire for control appeared to have played a role in how these subjects had gambled.

There also was some evidence that desire for control affected how much the subjects gambled. Desire for control scores predicted how much subjects had bet during their worst year of gambling, $r = .38$, and how much they had bet as a function of their annual income, $r = .40$. That is, the higher the level of desire for control, the more money the gamblers had bet.

But does this suggest that a higher desire for control was a cause of these peoples' problem gambling? Frankly, the findings surprised us. We compared the gamblers' DC Scale scores with those of the matched control group. The Gamblers Anonymous members had desire for control scores that were significantly *lower* than the control group. This finding was, of course, contrary to our predictions. It suggests that, at least with this group of subjects, a high desire for control was probably not a factor in the development of the problem gambling. Naturally, even without the nagging questions about the representativeness of the sample, there is the question of how the experience of hitting bottom and going through whatever treatment they had received affected the desire for control scores of these subjects. Nonetheless, the data certainly do not support the notion that a high desire for control contributes to problem gambling.

I also examined real gambling behavior in two additional field studies (Burger, 1991b). In both cases, I used legal gambling events, again with the cautionary note that the subjects I studied may not be representative of typical or problem gamblers. Nonetheless, this research is an improvement over the Burger and Smith (1985) study with the Gamblers Anonymous members in that all of the subjects were currently engaged in gambling behavior.

Subjects in the first study were adults who had just finished playing the California Lotto game. The California Lotto drawing is held each Wednesday and Saturday evening. At the time of the study, players paid one dollar to select six numbers from 1 to 49. Several million dollars can be won if the player's six numbers match the six selected in the next drawing. The odds of selecting all six numbers are 1 in 13,983,816. Of particular importance here, subjects have a choice of selecting the numbers themselves or of allowing a computer to randomly select six numbers for them, a procedure known as the Quick Pick method. I reasoned that selecting numbers oneself was more likely to create an illusion of control, and hence be more appealing to high desire for control players, than allowing a machine to select the numbers.

Subjects were surveyed coming out of convenience stores just hours before the drawing on Wednesday and Saturday evenings. Those who had just played the lotto game and who agreed to participate completed a questionnaire. They were first asked if they had either chosen the lotto numbers themselves, used the Quick Pick method, or had done both. We also asked them to estimate how much money they had spent playing Lotto during the past month, to indicate how likely they thought it was that they would someday win a lot of money playing the game, and to complete the DC Scale.

As expected, subjects who selected their own numbers had significantly higher desire for control scores ($M = 111.9$) than those who allowed the machine to select some ($M = 103.3$) or all of their numbers ($M = 98.6$). Thus, as in the earlier study, the level of desire for control appeared to affect how subjects gambled. Gamblers with a high desire for control tended to prefer the game that provided them with the greatest illusion of control. But does this finding mean that the illusion of control in the lotto game made these high desire for control subjects more susceptible to gambling? Apparently not. I found a significant negative correlation between desire for control and the amount of money subjects reported spending on the lotto game in the last month, $r = -.23$.

Thus, when high desire for control people play lotto, they prefer the method that gives them at least a hint of personal control. However, they also are less likely than people with a low desire for control to spend their money playing lotto. The findings suggest that desire for control is related to how people play the California Lotto, but if desire for control predicts how much they play, the relationship is in the opposite direction of what I might have guessed from earlier research.

The second legalized gambling situation I studied was the behavior of people in legal bingo parlors (Burger, 1991b). Casual observation of patrons of these parlors suggested that many bingo players engage in superstitious behaviors, such as wearing good luck charms or sitting in lucky seats. How is desire for control related to superstitious behavior? This is an interesting question, in that a case can be made that either high desire for control people or low desire for control people are more likely to engage in such behavior. On the one hand, we could argue that high desire for control people are more likely to be superstitious. The reasoning behind this prediction is that these people want to exercise control over the outcome of the game. However, because players simply mark off numbers called by the person running the game, bingo games offer little in the way of an illusion of control. Perhaps high desire for control people therefore try to influence whether they win or not by wearing a lucky shirt or using a lucky marker.

However, I chose to make the opposite prediction. Relying on good luck charms and other magical devices seems counter to the pattern observed in high desire for control people in many other settings. Believing that the outcome of a game is dependent on the day of the week or a good-luck charm is to believe that the outcome of the game is outside one's own control. Moreover, relying on such superstitions is tantamount to relinquishing control to a greater power. As described in Chapter 7, high desire for control people are more reluctant than people with a low desire for control to relinquish control over events, even when doing so is likely to result in a better outcome (Burger, McWard, & LaTorre, 1989). Relinquishing control over the outcome of the bingo game to a lucky charm is similar to relinquishing control over selection of lotto numbers found in the earlier study. Thus, I predicted that low desire for control subjects would be more likely that high desire for control subjects to engage in superstitious behavior in the bingo parlor.

People attending an evening of bingo playing were asked to fill out a questionnaire as they entered the bingo parlor. The questionnaire asked what, if any, behaviors they engaged in to increase their chances of winning and how much they felt these behaviors helped. They also were asked the number of times they had gone to a bingo parlor to play bingo during the past month and, finally, to complete the DC Scale.

Did desire for control affect how these people played bingo? The answer appears to be yes. I found that 41.3% of the bingo players listed at least one superstitious behavior. As expected, these people had significantly lower desire for control scores ($M = 95.5$) than those people who did not engage in this behavior ($M = 104.6$). Further, among those reporting at least one superstitious behavior, I found a negative correlation between desire for control and how many superstitious behaviors they listed, $r = -.33$. Thus, more superstitious behaviors were used by people with a lower desire for control. Finally, among those using superstitious behavior, I found a significant correlation between desire for control and the extent to which the subjects believed the superstitious behavior helped them win, $r = -.43$. In short, the data indicate that desire for control was related to how people gambled, that is, how they used superstitious behavior while playing bingo.

The next question is whether desire for control is related to how much the bingo players gambled. There was a significant correlation between desire for control and how often people reported playing bingo during the past month, $r = .30$. However, to my surprise, the correlation indicates that the higher the desire for control score, the more frequently these subjects played bingo.

What do the results of these three studies with real gamblers tell us about the role of desire for control in gambling behavior? First, in all three studies desire for control scores were related to *how* people gambled. Gamblers with a high desire for control prefer games that provide them with at least a hint of control. They are more likely to bet on horse races than craps, choose their own lotto numbers rather than let a machine make the selection, and avoid relying on good luck charms to help them win at bingo. Do these high desire for control gamblers recognize their limited ability to control the outcome of the game? This remains an open question. For example, it is possible that lotto players with a high desire for control are quite aware that their odds of winning are no better if they choose the six numbers than if a machine does the picking. They may simply find it more fun to do the selecting themselves. On the other hand, the results of some of the laboratory experiments indicate that even presumably intelligent university students are susceptible to some surprisingly obvious illusions of control, such as believing they can control the outcome of coin tosses.

The more difficult question is if desire for control affects whether and how much people gamble. The data answering this question are mixed. A high desire for control was related to betting more money in the Gamblers Anonymous study, but these gamblers tended to have lower than average desire for control scores. Low desire for control subjects reported betting more money in the lotto study, but high desire for control subjects reported playing bingo more often. Because different measures were used and different types of gambling were examined in these studies, the findings are not necessarily contradictory. However, it is clear that some as-yet-unexamined variables must influence the way desire for control affects whether and how much people gamble.

SUMMARY

Research on the illusion of control indicates that under certain circumstances people come to believe they have some control over outcomes that are otherwise obviously determined by chance. The results of several laboratory experiments indicate that high desire for control people are more susceptible to the illusion of control than people with a low desire for control. In each case, high desire for control subjects bet more than low desire for control subjects bet in simulated gambling situations. This pattern suggests that desire for control might be related to real gambling behavior and may even play a role in the etiology of problem gambling.

However, research with real gamblers and actual gambling behavior suggests that the relationship between desire for control and gambling is not a simple one. Desire for control does appear to affect how people gamble. Once they have decided to gamble, high desire for control people tend to prefer games that provide some illusion of control. However, it is not clear that high desire for control people are any more likely to gamble than people with a low desire for control, or if they are more likely to bet excessively when gambling. The research reviewed in this chapter indicates that individual differences in desire for control are somehow tied to gambling behavior. But teasing out that role requires much more investigation, particularly with real gamblers betting in real gambling situations.

CHAPTER 10

CONCLUSIONS

It has now been more than a dozen years since I began researching individual differences in desire for control. Many of my predictions about the differences between high and low desire for control people have been supported, but a number of my initial expectations have not. I came to recognize somewhere during this work that my real interest, which surely has shown through in this book, was to better understand the high desire for control person rather than the low. At times I have been guilty of thinking of low desire for control people simply as those lacking this need. Nonetheless, looking back on more than a hundred studies conducted by me and dozens of other researchers, I think I can see a fairly consistent picture of this high desire for control individual I have been tracking all these years.

High desire for control people approach most events asking themselves whether they will be able to control what happens. They are not content to accept what life throws their way, but rather are highly motivated to influence their worlds. Unlike those scoring low on the DC Scale, high desire for control people are more likely to recognize, or at least believe they recognize, when they have control. As long as their need for control is met by a perception that they indeed are in control, they are content and productive people. But for high desire for control people, squaring their need for control with a perception of control may become a persistent effort. High desire for control people have probably picked up many tricks and techniques they rely on to bring their needed and perceived control levels into sync. They can use the skills they have developed over the years to complete the challenging task or control the awkward conversation. When problems arise, they take direct actions to rectify the situation and reassert their sense of control. On other occasions high desire for control people retain their sense of control by convincing themselves they have more control over events than they probably do.

Unfortunately, there is the down side to a high desire for control as well. When their high need to exercise control comes into conflict with the realities of the world, high desire for control people may experience more stress and more depression than lows. When in a crowded room, they experience more discomfort and crowding. Most high desire for control people eventually learn to deal with these problems relatively well, and in the long run probably have happier and more productive lives than lows. However, their continued vigilance and the never-ending struggle to maintain a sense of personal control is the price they pay for these advantages.

I think the scope of the research reported in this book also demonstrates a key point I developed in the first chapter, that desire for control can be thought of as a general individual difference variable that applies to a large number of events in a person's life. Whether you have a high or low desire for control will play a role in your personal relationships, how you deal with potential stressors, how much you achieve, and so on. I believe that the extent to which people want to control the events in their lives is a key personality variable accounting for a large number of differences among people in a large number of situations.

The remainder of this chapter will be devoted to research and questions that need to be addressed before attaining closure on a discussion of desire for control. First, I want to present some research on desire for control that does not easily fit elsewhere in the book. Second, I want to introduce some largely overlooked questions concerning the development and change of desire for control.

MISCELLANEOUS RESEARCH

Although the research described in the previous chapters paints a fairly detailed picture of the high desire for control person, researchers also have applied this personality variable to such varied areas as photography and hypnotic susceptibility. For the sake of closure, I briefly touch on that work here.

Henry and Solano (1983) conducted an intriguing study into the relationship between personality and photography. In particular, they were interested in whether individual differences were related to the types of photographs people take. Undergraduates were given a camera with a 36-exposure roll of film and instructed to wander about the campus taking photographs of whatever they pleased. Judges coded the content of the photographs into various categories and compared scores from these codings with a number of personality scale scores, including the DC Scale. They found a significant negative correlation ($r = -.50$) between desire for control and the number of photographs subjects took of "people and natural objects." That is, the higher a subject's desire for control, the less often he or she took pictures of, for example, people standing in front of trees. Because the researchers examined a large number of correlations and because the relationship was not predicted, chance would appear the most logical explanation for this finding. Nonetheless, the results allow for some interesting posthoc speculation.

Another fascinating study using the DC Scale was reported by Drake (1988). Subjects in this study responded to items on the DC Scale as well as the Internal and Chance Scales from Levenson's Locus of Control Scales (see Chapter 2). The key variable in this experiment was whether subjects completed the scales during left-hemisphere or right-hemisphere activation. This activation was manipulated by presenting the material via earphones to either the right or left ear only. Consistent with his expectations, Drake found high correlations between the three measures during the left-hemisphere activation, but relatively low correlations during right-hemisphere activation. This research is consistent with earlier findings indicating more consistency during left-hemisphere activation than right.

Finally, I conducted an experiment trying to relate desire for control to hypnotic susceptibility. I reasoned that people will be more or less responsive to the hypnotist's suggestions when they believe the hypnotic experience is consistent with their need for control. That is, high desire for control people should be relatively unmotivated to respond to hypnotic suggestions when they believe the hypnotist is in control of what happens to them. However, these same people might find hypnosis more appealing and be more willing to respond to suggestions when they believe that they control their level of hypnotic susceptibility.

Undergraduate subjects in this unpublished study were randomly assigned to three conditions. Some subjects were told that how well they responded to the hypnotist's suggestions was largely up to them. Other subjects heard that their responsiveness was largely controlled by the hypnotist. A comparison group given neither of these descriptions also was included in the study. Subjects then were tested for their hypnotic susceptibility using the Harvard Group Scale of Hypnotic Susceptibility (Shor & Orne, 1962). Unfortunately, the predicted interaction between desire for control and instruction condition was not found. However, an internal analysis did provide some support for the hypothesis. I divided subjects via a median split on a manipulation check item into those who generally felt that hypnotic susceptibility was under their control and those who felt it was under the hypnotist's control. Consistent with my original expectations, I found high desire for control subjects in all conditions were more responsive to hypnotic suggestions than lows when they felt they controlled the experience and less responsive than lows when they felt the hypnotist was in control. Admittedly, the internal analysis makes the support for the prediction rather weak. However, the findings suggest yet one more area of interest to psychologists that might be affected by the subjects' desire for control levels.

DEVELOPMENTAL ISSUES

One of the biggest gaps in our picture of the high desire for control person concerns developmental issues. Why do some people develop a high desire for control, while others are low in this trait? How susceptible to change is a person's desire for control level? Although data are scarce, I can make some observations and a few guesses about the answers to these questions.

CHILDHOOD EXPERIENCES AND DESIRE FOR CONTROL

Where do individual differences in desire for control come from? In recent years personality psychologists have increasingly recognized the important role genetics plays in shaping adult personalities. Unfortunately, I have no data on the heritability of desire for control. Therefore, while acknowledging that future researchers may identify some genetic predisposition that influences the development of desire for control, I will limit my discussion to possible environmental determinants.

The most logical starting point in this discussion is an examination of experiences during one's development, with particular emphasis on parental and family styles. At least two general hypotheses can be advanced. The first is similar to that advocated by Alfred Adler in describing his notion of striving for superiority (see Chapter 1). Adler maintained that this incessant need to demonstrate one's superiority over other people and all challenges results from feelings of inferiority in childhood. Thus, the more helpless a person feels in early childhood, the greater the striving for superiority. From this perspective, we might guess that an adult with a high desire for control experienced a lack of control over many of the events he or she encountered as a child. In other words, persistent frustration in one's ability to exercise control as a child might lead to a high need for control in adults.

This analysis is similar to that provided by psychologists working with adult children of alcoholics, as described in Chapter 7. Many children with one or more alcoholic parent grow up in homes that are highly uncontrollable and unpredictable. They may be unable to control or predict when Dad will hug them or hit them. These children respond to this situation by developing a strong need to exercise control over those things in their lives that they can control. This high need for control may continue in adulthood. Consequently, many psychologists have identified a high need for control as characteristic of many of the adult children of alcoholics they see in their practices (Brown, 1988).

However, when examined from another view, a case can also be made that high desire for control people experienced a great deal of control during their childhood years. One could argue from a behavioral or social learning perspective that high desire for control adults frequently were allowed to make their own decisions and feel responsible for their own actions as they grew up. Influencing others, making their own decisions, and taking charge of a situation were reinforced and became part of their personality.

Thus, a case can be made that either a deprivation of control or extensive experience with control results in a high desire for control. The only effort I have made to examine this question was a relatively simple study conducted with a student, Randy Husbands. We administered a questionnaire to 61 undergraduates who had taken the DC Scale earlier. The questionnaire contained 58 statements that we guessed might be related to either a perceived lack of control in childhood or a sense of control and autonomy, as guided by the two hypotheses (for example, "How often were you allowed to select which clothes you wanted to wear?"). Subjects were asked to respond to the items by thinking about their parents or the people who served as parents when they were between 6 and 12 years old. Each of these items was answered on a nine-point scale.

Because the study was exploratory, we simply divided subjects into high and low desire for control halves and looked at which items seemed to discriminate between the two groups at the .05 level or better. The results are presented in Table 10-1. A glance at the items in the table suggests that high desire for control subjects were more likely than lows to grow up in a home in which parents were encouraging, not controlling. Further, while these high desire for control subjects were more likely to play with children in the neighborhood and school, they did not remember having more close friends than the low desire for control subjects. This latter finding is particularly interesting when compared with the research reported in Chapter 3, in which adult high desire for control subjects also report having and preferring fewer close friends

TABLE 10-1. Items Discriminating between
High Desire for Control Subjects and Low Desire for Control Subjects

	High desire for control	Low desire for control
Items rated higher by high desire for control subjects		
To what degree did your parents encourage you to make new friends at school or in the neighborhood?	6.71	5.40
To what degree did your parents take you places with them (e.g., restaurants, movies, trips)?	7.81	6.67
To what extent were you accepted by other children in your neighborhood or class?	7.58	6.73
To what extent was your mother generally satisfied with her life and work?	7.39	6.57
To what extent did your parents praise you for your extracurricular school activities?	7.48	6.33
How often did you participate in playground games?	7.94	7.17
Items rated higher by low desire for control subjects		
How structured did your parents make your day?	3.60	4.87
How many close friends did you generally have?	3.35	4.30
How often did you ask for help with projects (e.g., building model cars, baking a cake, assembling a puzzle, doing your homework)?	3.57	5.27

than lows. Of course, we cannot know from this retrospective procedure whether subjects could accurately recall their number of close childhood friends or if they merely reflected on their current preferences.

As part of our initial efforts to understand the backgrounds of high and low desire for control adults, we also asked the subjects in this study if their parents had been divorced, how many siblings they grew up with, and their birth order position. However, none of these variables came close to differentiating high and low desire for control subjects.

Although the data reported in Table 10-1 are just exploratory, they do seem to support the behavioral and social learning explanation over the Adlerian model. The high desire for control subjects in this study did not recall more feelings of helplessness and dependence in their childhoods than the lows. However, research in other areas suggests that the relationship between parental behavior and desire for control is probably more complex than this two-hypothesis question suggests.

Some of this complexity has been described by Eccles, Buchanan, Flanagan, Fuligni, Midgley, and Yee (in press). These researchers argue that the child's need for structure and need for autonomy change as he or she matures. In particular, the child's need for autonomy grows as he or she enters early adolescence. Data from Eccles *et al.* (in press) suggest that intrinsic motivation for academic work suffers when the child's increased need for autonomy is frustrated by parents and teachers. The researchers found that junior high school students allowed an opportunity to be involved in decision making at home and in school had the highest levels of intrinsic interest in their school work. Moreover, they found maturation rates for autonomy needs may be different for males and females.

Similarly, Rothbaum and Weisz (1989) explain that control means different things to children at different ages. Whereas young children think of control simply in terms of causes leading to effects, older children are more likely to concentrate on power and freedom as indicators of control. These researchers also maintain that childrens' efforts to exercise control can develop into problem behaviors and that these vary as a function of age. Attempts to gain a sense of personal control might be expressed as interpersonal aggression or passivity in young children, but as rebellion and depression in adolescents.

All of this research suggests that it may not be easy to identify a single parental style that leads to high or low desire for control adults. Rather, parents may need to adapt the amount of structure they impose and the amount of independence they allow to the child's changing needs. Moreover, there may be more than one route to a high desire for control. That is, it is possible that either parental encouragement to be independent or a perceived lack of control in childhood could lead to a high desire for control. It also remains an open question as to when individual differences in desire for control are formed. Heft *et al.* (1988) modified the DC Scale for use with children and report reasonable internal consistencies for samples of children as young as fifth grade. Their modified scale would seem to be particularly useful in future research examining the development of desire for control. The link between childhood experiences and adult desire for control level will remain highly speculative until more research with more sophisticated methods is conducted.

CHANGING DESIRE FOR CONTROL LEVEL

I have assumed that desire for control, like other personality traits, is fairly stable over time. The test–retest data reported in Chapter 2 for periods of up to one year support this assumption. However, personality trait researchers also acknowledge that individual differences are subject to change, particularly slow changes over long periods of time or changes brought about by dramatic personal experiences. Thus, one remaining question concerns how desire for control level might change in adults.

The only relevant data I have on this question was uncovered in the recent longitudinal investigation reported in Chapter 2 (Burger & Solano, 1991). Males who completed the DC Scale as undergraduates in 1980 showed very little change in their desire for control when they completed the scale again in 1990. However, the average female in the sample showed a dramatic increase in her desire for control during that 10-year period.

Although there are many possible explanations for this finding, one that I find particularly appealing at this point concerns the experiences these women had after leaving college. The subjects were all students at Wake Forest University in North Carolina in 1980. Most of the females in the sample had come from rather protected environments and had grown up in relatively conservative homes. Thus, we should not have been too surprised to find that these women reflected the stereotypic traits of dependent and yielding women that were prevalent during their gender–role socialization. However, as these women graduated and entered the business and professional worlds, they may have discovered the value (perhaps the necessity) of exercising control over the events in their lives. Getting ahead in their careers and other areas of their lives may have required that they become more assertive and less dependent. Exercising control and being reinforced for this behavior may have led to an increase in these women's desire for control generally. Although this interpretation is highly speculative, it is consistent with the earlier suggestion that a high desire for control is more likely to develop in a home where parents encourage and reward their children's independence and autonomy. The data from the 20- to 30-year-old women in the Burger and Solano (1991) study indicate that these experiences might also effectively alter the desire for control scores of adults.

THE LARGER PICTURE

After working with a construct for as long as I have been studying desire for control, it is easy to fall into the trap of explaining any and all psychological phenomena in terms of that construct. Consequently, I often find myself reading a journal article or listening to a talk and thinking something like "I bet that only works for high desire for control people," or "The reason people do that is to satisfy their need for control." And although I know this is partly a function of my own intense interest in the topic, I often find a similar reaction in other psychologists and students who hear me talk about or who read about my work. "I wonder if desire for control might not be related to . . ." they tell me. Almost invariably, I tell them I think it might.

Although I recognize that personality and human behavior are more complex than a single individual difference variable, like some of the theorists reviewed in the first chapter, I also continue to believe that a motivation to control one's environment is very central to human functioning. Human nature tells us that events are caused and that we often, but not always, are capable of determining much of what happens to us. When B. F. Skinner (1971) argued that freedom and dignity are largely illusory, most people seemed to reject that extreme position not because they could demonstrate that it was untrue, but rather because they did not want to believe it. Accurately or not, we want to believe that our behavior is determined by personal choices rather than it being the result of operant and classical conditioning. Although we can identify situations in which personal control is not desired (Burger, 1989a), we all have a need to feel some control over what happens to us. Because this need for control is ubiquitous, we should not be surprised to find that individual differences in desire for control play a role in a large number of situations.

Perhaps this is why I have found a great deal of interest in desire for control from professionals outside of psychology. For example, an economist told me that he no longer believes that business executives are primarily motivated to keep a healthy bottom line for the corporation. Rather, he explained that the typical business person is motivated by a personal need to exercise control and feel powerful. A man or woman satisfies this need not only by climbing the corporate ladder, but by making corporate decisions in a way that maximizes the amount of personal control that person retains over the corporation and its personnel. This economist maintained that when an executive is forced to select between what is good for the company and what is good for his or her need for control, the choice will almost always be the one that satisfies the need for control. Not only did this man seem to be saying much of what I would have said if I had studied this area, he even used the expression *desire for control* before I could.

Conversations with educators, health professionals, parents, and others have reinforced my belief that desire for control has implications far beyond those explored in this book. An elementary school teacher explained to me that one of the most important things she can do for her students is keep alive their intrinsic interest in exploring and learning to control their worlds. A physician told me that, after more than thirty years of practice, he believes his patients' health is more under their control than his. The patients who take control over their own health care and see him only as a resource in this effort are the ones who remain healthy. And as a Little League manager I have seen that the joy the children get from playing the game lies in the sense of mastery and accomplishment that comes from making a difficult catch or hitting the ball farther than seemed possible, rather than from the team's won–loss record.

In summary, the motivation to exercise control is a ubiquitous feature of our daily experience. Because the need for control touches so many important parts of our lives, individual differences in desire for control will account for some of the variance in much of what we do. The variety of topics explored in this book attests to the widespread applicability of desire for control. However, if I am correct about the central role motivation for control plays in human behavior, the research conducted on desire for control to date may have only scratched the surface.

SUMMARY

More than a dozen years of examining individual differences in desire for control have convinced me that this personality variable is one of the most pervasive and important of those studied by personality researchers. The extent to which people want to feel in control of the events in their lives would seem to play an important role in behaviors examined by psychologists in many different areas. This broad application is illustrated not only by the wide variety of topics covered in the previous chapters, but by the miscellaneous research reported here, such as that dealing with photography and hypnotic susceptibility.

One of the big gaps in desire for control research concerns developmental and change issues. A case can be made that a high desire for control can result from either experiences with a lack of control in childhood, or a childhood in which exercising control was possible and encouraged. Some recent data indicate that desire for control levels can change in adulthood, probably as a result of changing environments and demands to exercise control.

REFERENCES

Abramson, L. Y., Seligman, M. E .P., & Teasdale, J. D. (1978). Learned helplessness in humans: Critique and reformulation. *Journal of Abnormal Psychology, 87*, 49–74.

Adler, A. (1930). Individual psychology. In C. Murchison (Ed.), *Psychologies of 1930* (pp. 138–165). Worcester, MA: Clark University Press.

Alloy, L. B. & Abramson, L. Y. (1979). Judgment of contingency in depressed and non-depressed students: Sadder but wiser? *Journal of Experimental Psychology: General, 108*, 441–485.

Altman, I. & Taylor, D. A. (1973). *Social penetration: The development of interpersonal relationships.* New York: Holt, Rinehart & Winston.

Ansbacher, H. L. & Ansbacher, R. R. (Eds.) (1956). *The individual psychology of Alfred Alder.* New York: Basic Books.

Argyle, M. (1987). *The psychology of happiness.* London: Methuen.

Aron, A. & Aron, E. N. (1986). *The heart of social psychology.* Lexington, MA: Lexington Books.

Asch, S. E. (1951). Effects of group pressure upon the modification and distortion of judgments. In H. Guetzkow (Ed.), *Groups, leadership, and men* (pp. 177–190). Pittsburgh, PA: Carnegie Press.

Bandura, A. (1977). Self-efficacy: Toward a unifying theory of behavioral change. *Psychological Review, 84*, 191–215.

Bandura, A. (1986). *Social foundations of thought and action: A social cognitive theory.* Englewood Cliffs, NJ: Prentice-Hall.

Barber, J. G., Winefield, A. H., & Mortimer, K. (1986). The Personal Interest Questionnaire: A task-specific measure of locus of control and motivation for use in learned helplessness research. *Personality and Individual Differences, 7*, 311–318.

Beck, A. T. (1972). *Depression: Causes and treatments.* Philadelphia: University of Pennsylvania Press.

Bem, S. L. (1974). The measurement of psychological androgyny. *Journal of Consulting and Clinical Psychology, 42*, 155–162.

Benassi, V. A., Sweeney, P. D., & Dufour, C. L. (1988). Is there a relationship between locus of control orientation and depression? *Journal of Abnormal Psychology, 97*, 357–367.

Berkowitz, A. & Perkins, H. W. (1988). Personality characteristics of children of alcoholics. *Journal of Consulting and Clinical Psychology, 56*, 206–209.

181

Binik, Y. M. (1985). Psychosocial predictors of sudden death: A review and critique. *Social Science and Medicine, 20,* 667–680.

Bradburn, N. (1969). *The structure of psychological well-being.* Chicago: Aldine.

Braith, J. A., McCullough, J. P., & Bush, J. P. (1988). Relaxation-induced anxiety in a subclinical sample of chronically anxious subjects. *Journal of Behavior Therapy and Experimental Psychiatry, 19,* 193–198.

Braukmann, W. (1981). *Darstellung eines Bezugsrahmens zum Konzept der Kontrollmotivation und Entwicklung einer deutschsprachungen Version der "Desirability of Control Scale" von Burger and Cooper* (Forschungsbericht Nr. 12). University of Trier, Germany.

Brehm, J. W. (1966). *A theory of psychological reactance.* New York: Academic.

Brehm, S. S. & Brehm, J. W. (1981). *Psychological reactance: A theory of freedom and control.* New York: Academic.

Brehm, S. S. & Smith, T. W. (1986). Social psychological approaches to psychotherapy and behavior change. In S. L. Garfield & A. E. Bergin (Eds.), *Handbook of psychotherapy and behavior change* (3rd ed., pp. 69–115). New York: Wiley.

Breslow, N. (1987). Locus of control, desirability of control, and sadomasochists. *Psychological Reports, 61,* 995–1001.

Brown, S. (1988). *Treating adult children of alcoholics: A developmental perspective.* New York: Wiley.

Burger, J. M. (1980). *Effectance motivation and the overjustification effect.* Unpublished doctoral dissertation, University of Missouri–Columbia, Columbia, MO.

Burger, J. M. (1984). Desire for control, locus of control, and proneness to depression. *Journal of Personality, 52,* 71–89.

Burger, J. M. (1985). Desire for control and achievement-related behaviors. *Journal of Personality and Social Psychology, 48,* 1520–1533.

Burger, J. M. (1986). Desire for control and the illusion of control: The effects of familiarity and sequence of outcomes. *Journal of Research in Personality, 20,* 66–76.

Burger, J. M. (1987a). Desire for control and conformity to a perceived norm. *Journal of Personality and Social Psychology, 53,* 355–360.

Burger, J. M. (1987b). Increased performance with increased personal control: A self-presentation interpretation. *Journal of Experimental Social Psychology, 23,* 350–360.

Burger, J. M. (1987c). The effects of desire for control on attributions and task performance. *Basic and Applied Social Psychology, 8,* 309–320.

Burger, J. M. (1989a). Negative reactions to increases in perceived personal control. *Journal of Personality and Social Psychology, 56,* 246–256.

Burger, J. M. (1989b). *Need for privacy: Theory and measurement.* Unpublished manuscript.

Burger, J. M. (1990). Desire for control and interpersonal interaction style. *Journal of Research in Personality, 24,* 32–44.

Burger, J. M. (1991a). *Desire for control and academic achievement.* Paper presented at the annual meeting of the American Psychological Association, San Francisco.

Burger, J. M. (1991b). The effects of desire for control in situations with chance-determined outcomes: Gambling behavior in lotto and bingo players. *Journal of Research in Personality, 25,* 196–204.

Burger, J. M. & Arkin, R. M. (1980). Prediction, control and learned helplessness. *Journal of Personality and Social Psychology, 38,* 482–491.

Burger, J. M. & Burns, L. (1988). The illusion of unique invulnerability and the use of effective contraception. *Personality and Social Psychology Bulletin, 14,* 264–270.

Burger, J. M. & Cooper, H. M. (1979). The desirability of control. *Motivation and Emotion, 3,* 381–393.

Burger, J. M. & Hemans, L. T. (1988). Desire for control and the use of attribution processes. *Journal of Personality, 56*, 531–546.

Burger, J. M., McWard, J., & LaTorre, D. (1989). Boundaries of self-control: Relinquishing control over aversive events. *Journal of Social and Clinical Psychology, 8*, 209–221.

Burger, J. M., Oakman, J. A., & Bullard, N. G. (1983). Desire for control and the perception of crowding. *Personality and Social Psychology Bulletin, 9*, 475–479.

Burger, J. M. & Schnerring, D. A. (1982). The effects of desire for control and extrinsic rewards on the illusion of control and gambling. *Motivation and Emotion, 6*, 329–335.

Burger, J. M. & Smith, N. G. (1985). Desire for control and gambling behavior among problem gamblers. *Personality and Social Psychology Bulletin, 11*, 145–152.

Burger, J. M. & Solano, C. H. (1991). *Gender differences in desire for control: A ten-year longitudinal study.* Paper presented at the annual meeting of the American Psychological Association, San Francisco.

Burger, J. M. & Vartabedian, R. A. (1980). Desire for control and reaction to proattitudinal and counterattitudinal arguments. *Motivation and Emotion, 4*, 239–246.

Cacioppo, J. T., Petty, R. E., & Kao, C. F. (1984). The efficient assessment of need for cognition. *Journal of Personality Assessment, 48*, 306–307.

Cacioppo, J. T., Petty, R. E., Kao, C. F., & Rodriguez, R. (1986). Central and peripheral routes to persuasion: An individual difference perspective. *Journal of Personality and Social Psychology, 51*, 1032–1043.

Christie, R., & Geis, F. L. (1970). *Studies in Machiavellianism.* New York: Academic.

Costello, C. G. (1978). A critical review of Seligman's laboratory experiments on learned helplessness and depression in humans. *Journal of Abnormal Psychology, 87*, 21–31.

Crandall, V. C., Katkovsky, W., & Crandall, V. (1965). Children's beliefs in their own control of reinforcements in intellectual-academic situations. *Child Development, 36*, 91–109.

Crowe, C. M. & Burger, J. M. (1984). *Locus of control, desire for control, and proneness to depression.* Paper presented at the annual meeting of the Southeastern Psychological Association, New Orleans.

Daubman, K. A. (1990). *The self-threat of receiving help: A comparison of the threat-to-self-esteem model and the threat-to-interpersonal-power model.* Unpublished manuscript, Gettysburg College, Gettysburg, PA.

Davis, J. D. (1976). Self-disclosure in an acquaintance exercise: Responsibility for level of intimacy. *Journal of Personality and Social Psychology, 33*, 787–792.

deCharms, R. (1968). *Personal causation: The internal affective determinants of behavior.* New York: Academic.

Deci, E. L. (1975). *Intrinsic motivation.* New York: Plenum.

Deci, E. L. (1980). *The psychology of self-determination.* Lexington, MA: Lexington Books.

Deci, E. L. & Ryan, R. M. (1985a). *Intrinsic motivation and self-determination in human behavior.* New York: Plenum.

Deci, E. L. & Ryan, R. M. (1985b). The General Causality Orientations Scale: Self-determination in personality. *Journal of Research in Personality, 19*, 109–134.

Deci, E. L. & Ryan, R. M. (1987). The support of autonomy and the control of behavior. *Journal of Personality and Social Psychology, 53*, 1024–1037.

Dembroski, T. M., & Costa, P. T. (1987). Coronary-prone behavior: Components of the Type A pattern and hostility. *Journal of Personality, 55*, 211–235.

Dembroski, T. M., MacDougall, J. M., & Musante, L. (1984). Desirability of control versus locus of control: Relationship to paralinguistics in the Type A interview. *Health Psychology, 3*, 15–26.

Derlega, V. J. & Berg, J. H. (Eds.). (1987). *Self-disclosure: Theory, research, and therapy.* New York: Plenum.

Drake, R. A. (1987). Conceptions of own versus others' outcomes: Manipulation of nonaural attentional orientation. *European Journal of Social Psychology, 17,* 373–375.

Drake, R. A. (1988). Cognitive style induced by hemisphere priming: Consistent versus inconsistent self-report. *Bulletin of the Psychonomic Society, 26,* 313–315.

Eccles, J. S., Buchanan, C. M., Flanagan, C., Fuligni, A., Midgley, C., & Yee, D. (in press). Control and autonomy: Individuation revisited in early adolescence. *Journal of Social Issues.*

Edwards, A. L. (1959). *Manual for the Edwards Personal Preference Schedule.* New York: The Psychological Corporation.

Engel, G. L. (1971). Sudden and rapid death during psychological stress: Folklore or folk wisdom? *Annals of Internal Medicine, 74,* 771–782.

Eysenck, H. J. (1982). Development of a theory. In C. D. Spielberger (Ed.), *Personality, genetics and behavior* (pp. 1–38). New York: Praeger.

Eysenck, H. J. & Eysenck, S. B. G. (1968). *Manual for the Eysenck Personality Inventory.* San Diego: Educational and Industrial Testing Service.

Feinberg, R. A., Powell, A., & Miller, F. G. (1982). Control and belief in the just world: What's good also can be bad. *Social Behavior and Personality, 10,* 57–61.

Fletcher, G. J. O., Danilovics, P., Fernandez, G., Peterson, D., & Reeder, G. D. (1986). Attributional complexity: An individual differences measure. *Journal of Personality and Social Psychology, 51,* 875–884.

Folkman, S. (1984). Personal control and stress and coping processes: a theoretical analysis. *Journal of Personality and Social Psychology, 46,* 839–852.

Friedman, M., & Rosenman, R. (1974). *Type A behavior and your heart.* New York: Knopf.

Funder, D. C. (1987). Errors and mistakes: Evaluating the accuracy of social judgment. *Psychological Bulletin, 101,* 75–90.

Ganong, L. H., & Coleman, M. (1987). Sex roles and yielded/expressed self-control. *Sex Roles, 16,* 401–408.

Gilbert, D. T. (1989). Thinking lightly about others: Automatic components of the social inference process. In J. S. Uleman & J. A. Bargh (Eds.), *Unintended thought* (pp. 189–211). New York: Guilford.

Glass, D. C. (1977). *Behavior patterns, stress, and coronary diesease.* Hillsdale, NH: Erlbaum.

Hatton, D. C., Gilden, E. R., Edwards, M. E., Cutler, J., Kron, J., & McAnulty, J. H. (1989). Psychophysiological factors in ventricular arrhythmias and sudden cardiac death. *Journal of Psychosomatic Research, 33,* 621–631.

Hayes, M. E. (1988). *A motivational model of gambling behavior.* Unpublished Master's Thesis, Southern Connecticut State University, New Haven, CT.

Heft, L., Thoresen, C. E., Kirmil-Gray, K., Wiedenfeld, S. A., Eagleston, J. R., Bracke, P., & Arnow, B. (1988). Emotional and temperamental correlates of Type A in children and adolescents. *Journal of Youth and Adolescence, 17,* 461–475.

Hegarty, W. H. & Sims, H. P. (1978). Some determinants of unethical decision behavior: An experiment. *Journal of Applied Psychology, 63,* 451–457.

Heide, F. J. & Borkovec, T. D. (1983). Relaxation-induced anxiety: Paradoxical anxiety enhancement due to relaxation training. *Journal of Consulting and Clinical Psychology, 51,* 171–182.

Henry, W. P. & Solano, C. H. (1983). Photographic style and personality: Developing a coding system for photographs. *Journal of Psychology, 115,* 79–87.

Hiroto, D. S. (1974). Locus of control and learned helplessness. *Journal of Experimental Psychology, 102,* 187–193.

Hiroto, D. S. & Seligman, M. E. P. (1975). Generality of learned helplessness in man. *Journal of Personality and Social Psychology, 31,* 311–327.

Hojat, M. & Crandall, R. (Eds.) (1987). Special issue: Loneliness: Theory, research and applications. *Journal of Social Behavior and Personality 2*(2).

Holahan, C. J. & Moos, R. H. (1987). Personal and contextual determinants of coping strategies. *Journal of Personality and Social Psychology, 52*, 949–955.

Kelley, H. H. (1971). *Attributions in social interaction*. Morristown, NJ: General Learning Press.

Kluger, A. (1988). Unpublished data.

Kobasa, S. C. (1979). Stressful life events, personality, and health: An inquiry into hardiness. *Journal of Personality and Social Psychology, 37*, 1–11.

Langer, E. J. (1975). The illusion of control. *Journal of Personality and Social Psychology, 32*, 311–328.

Langer, E. J. & Roth, J. (1975). Heads I win, tails it's chance: The illusion of control as a function of the sequence of outcomes in a purely chance task. *Journal of Personality and Social Psychology, 32*, 951–955.

Lawler, K. A., Schmied, L. A., Armstead, C. A., & Lacy, J. E. (1990). Type A behavior, desire for control, and cardiovascular reactivity in young adult women. *Journal of Social Behavior and Personality, 5*, 135–158.

Lazarus, R. S. & Folkman, S. (1984). *Stress, appraisal and coping*. New York: Springer.

Leak, G. K. (1985). Unpublished data.

Leary, M. R. (1983). Social anxiousness: The construct and its measurement. *Journal of Personality Assessment, 47*, 66–75.

Lepper, M. R. & Greene, D. (1978). Overjustification research and beyond: Toward a means-ends analysis of intrinsic and extrinsic motivation. In M. R. Lepper & D. Greene (Eds.) *The hidden costs of rewards: New perspectives on the psychology of human motivation* (pp. 109–148). Hillsdale, NJ: Erlbaum.

Lerner, M. J. & Miller, D. T. (1978). Just world research and the attribution process: Looking back and ahead. *Psychological Bulletin, 85*, 1030–1051.

Levenson, H. (1981). Differentiating among internality, powerful others, and chance. In H. M. Lefcourt (Ed.), *Research with the locus of control construct: Vol. 1. Assessment methods* (pp. 15–63). New York: Academic.

Lewinsohn, P. M., Mischel, W., Chaplin, W., & Barton, R. (1980). Social competence and depression: The role of illusory self perceptions. *Journal of Abnormal Psychology, 89*, 203–212.

Liu, T. J. & Steele, C. M. (1986). Attributional analysis as self-affirmation. *Journal of Personality and Social Psychology, 51*, 531–540.

Matthews, K. A. & Haynes, S. G. (1986). Type A behavior pattern and coronary risk: Update and critical evaluation. *American Journal of Epidemiology, 123*, 923–960.

Miller, I. W. & Norman, W. H. (1979). Learned helplessness in humans: A review and attribution theory model. *Psychological Bulletin, 86*, 93–118.

Murray, H. A. (1938). *Explorations in personality: A clinical and experimental study of fifty men of college age*. New York: Oxford University Press.

Musante, L., MacDougall, J. M., Dembroski, T. M., & Van Horn, A. E. (1983). Component analysis of the Type A coronary-prone behavior pattern in male and female college students. *Journal of Personality and Social Psychology, 45*, 1104–1117.

Nadler, A. (1986). Self-esteem and the seeking and receiving of help: Theoretical and empirical perspectives. In B. A. Maher & W. B. Maher (Eds.), *Progress in experimental personality research* (Vol. 14, pp. 115–163). New York: Academic.

Nadler, A., & Fisher, J. D. (1986). The role of threat to self-esteem and perceived control in recipient reaction to help: Theory development and empirical validations. In L.

Berkowitz (Ed.), *Advances in experimental social psychology* (Vol. 19, pp. 81–122). New York: Academic.

Nunnally, J. C. (1967). *Psychometric theory.* New York: McGraw-Hill.

Pardine, P., Napoli, A., & Dytell, R. (1983). *Health-behavior change mediating the stress-illness relationship.* Paper presented at the annual meeting of the American Psychological Association, Anaheim, CA.

Paulhus, D. (1983). Sphere-specific measures of perceived control. *Journal of Personality and Social Psychology, 44,* 1253–1265.

Peplau, L. A. & Perlman, D. (1982). *Loneliness: A sourcebook of current theory, research and therapy.* New York: Wiley.

Perlmuter, L. C. & Monty, R. A. (1977). The importance of perceived control: Fact or fantasy? *American Scientist, 65,* 759–765.

Perloff, L. S. & Fetzer, B. K. (1986). Self-other judgments and perceived vulnerability to victimization. *Journal of Personality and Social Psychology, 50,* 502–510.

Peterson, C., Semmel, A., von Baeyer, C., Abramson, L. Y., Metalsky, G. I., & Seligman, M. E. P. (1982). The Attributional Style Questionnaire. *Cognitive Therapy and Research, 6,* 287–300.

Peterson, C., Villanova, P., & Raps, C. S. (1985). Depression and attributions: Factors responsible for inconsistent results in the published literature. *Journal of Abnormal Psychology, 94,* 165–168.

Pittman, T. S. & Pittman, N. L. (1980). Deprivation of control and the attribution process. *Journal of Personality and Social Psychology, 39,* 377–389.

Prewett, M., Spence, R., & Chaknis, M. (1981). Attribution of causality by children with alcoholic parents. *International Journal of the Addictions, 16,* 367–370.

Radloff, L. S. (1977). The CES-D Scale: A self-report depression scale for research in the general population. *Applied Psychological Measurement, 1,* 385–401.

Reed, T. F. (1989). Do union organizers matter? Individual differences, campaign practices, and representation election outcomes. *Industrial and Labor Relations Review, 43,* 103–119.

Reid, D. W. (1984). Participatory control and the chronic-illness adjustment process. In H. M. Lefcourt (Ed.), *Research with the locus of control construct: Vol. 2. Extensions and limitations* (pp. 361–389). New York: Academic.

Rhodewalt, F. & Marcroft, M. (1988). Type A behavior and diabetic control: Implications of psychological reactance for health outcomes. *Journal of Applied Social Psychology, 18,* 139–159.

Robins, C. J. (1988). Attributions and depression: Why is the literature so inconsistent? *Journal of Personality and Social Psychology, 54,* 880–889.

Rodin, J., Rennert, K., & Solomon, S. K. (1980). Intrinsic motivation for control: Fact or fiction. In A. Baum & J. E. Singer (Eds.), *Advances in environmental psychology: Vol 2. Applications of personal control* (pp. 131–148). Hillsdale, NJ: Erlbaum.

Rodin, J., Solomon, S. K., & Metcalf, J. (1978). Role of control in mediating perceptions of density. *Journal of Personality and Social Psychology, 36,* 988–999.

Rosenberg, M. (1965). *Society and the adolescent self-image.* Princeton, NJ: Princeton University Press.

Rosenman, R. H. (1978). The interview method of assessment of the coronary-prone behavior pattern. In T. M. Dembroski, S. M. Weiss, J. L. Shields, S. G. Haynes, & M. Feinleib (Eds.), *Coronary-prone behavior* (pp. 269–279). New York: Springer-Verlag.

Roth, S. (1980). A revised model of learned helplessness in humans. *Journal of Personality, 48,* 103–133.

Rothbaum, F. & Weisz, J. R. (1989). *Child psychopathology and the quest for control.* Newbury Park, CA: Sage.

Rothbaum, F., Weisz, J. R., & Snyder, S. S. (1982). Changing the world and changing the self: A two-process model of perceived control. *Journal of Personality and Social Psychology, 42,* 5–37.

Rotter, J. B. (1966). Generalized expectancies for internal versus external control of reinforcement. *Psychological Monographs, 80* (1, Whole No. 609).

Rubin, Z. & Peplau, A. (1975). Belief in a just world and reactions to another's lot: A study of participants in the national draft lottery. *Journal of Social Issues, 29,* 73–93.

Russell, D., Peplau, L. A., & Cutrona, C. E. (1980). The revised UCLA Loneliness Scale: Concurrent and discriminant validity. *Journal of Personality and Social Psychology, 39,* 472–480.

Ryan, L. R. (1970). *Clinical interpretation of the FIRO-B.* Palo Alto, CA: Consulting Psychologists Press.

Ryland, E. & Levy, S. (1988). *Occupational stress and the gender gap: An issue of control?* Unpublished manuscript, California State University, San Bernardino.

Santos, M. D. & Burger, J. M. (1988). *Desire for control and health.* Paper presented at the annual meeting of the Western Psychological Association, Burlingame, CA.

Scheier, M. F. & Carver, C. S. (1985). Optimism, coping, and health: Assessment and implications of generalized outcome expectancies. *Health Psychology, 4,* 219–247.

Schmidt, D. E. & Keating, J. P. (1979). Human crowding and personal control: An integration of the research. *Psychological Bulletin, 86,* 680–700.

Schmidt, N. & Sermat, V. (1983). Measuring loneliness in different relationships. *Journal of Personality and Social Psychology, 44,* 1038–1047.

Schönbach, P. (1990). *Account episodes: The management or escalation of conflict.* Cambridge: Cambridge University Press.

Schutz, W. (1977). *Instruction manual for the FIRO-B.* Palo Alto, CA: Consulting Psychologists Press.

Schwartz, M., Ripley, K., & Conrad, M. (1981). *The desirability of control: Its presence in married couples and its effect on mate selection.* Unpublished manuscript, Wake Forest University, Winston-Salem, NC.

Seligman, M. E. P. (1975). *Helplessness: On depression, development and death.* San Francisco: Freeman.

Shor, R. E. & Orne, M. T. (1962). *Harvard Group Scale of Hypnotic Susceptibility.* Palo Alto, CA: Consulting Psychologists Press.

Skinner, B. F. (1971). *Beyond freedom and dignity.* New York: Knopf.

Smith, R. A., Wallston, B. S., Wallston, K. A., Forsberg, P. R., & King, J. E. (1984). Measuring desire for control of health care processes. *Journal of Personality and Social Psychology, 47,* 415–426.

Smith, R. A. P., Woodward, N. J., Wallston, B. S., Wallston, K. A., Rye, P., & Zylstra, M. (1988). Health care implications of desire and expectancy for control in elderly adults. *Journal of Gerontology: Psychological Sciences, 43,* P1–P7.

Smith, T. W. & O'Keefe, J. L. (1985). The inequivalence of self-reports of Type A behavior: Differential relationships of the Jenkins Activity Survey and the Framingham Scale with affect, stress, and control. *Motivation and Emotion, 9,* 299–311.

Snyder, C. R. (1989). Reality negotiation: From excuses to hope and beyond. *Journal of Social and Clinical Psychology, 8,* 130–157.

Snyder, C. R., Harris, C., Anderson, J. R., Gibb, J., Yoshinobu, L., Langelle, C., Harney, P., Holleran, S., & Irving, L. M. (1989). *The development and validation of an individual difference measure of hope.* Paper presented at the annual meeting of the American Psychological Association, New Orleans.

Snyder, C. R., Harris, C., Anderson, J. R., Holleran, S. A., Irving, L. M., Sigmon, S. T.,

Yoshinobu, L., Gibb, J., Langelle, C., & Harney, P. (1991). The will and the ways: Development and validation of an individual-difference measure of hope. *Journal of Personality and Social Psychology, 60,* 570–585.

Solano, C. H. (1987). Loneliness and perceptions of control: General traits versus specific attributions. In M. Hojat & R. Crandall (Eds.), Loneliness: Theory, Research and Applications. *Journal of Social Behavior and Personality, 2*(2), 201–214.

Spence, J. T. & Helmreich, R. L. (1983). Acheivement-related motives and behaviors. In J. T. Spence (Ed.), *Achievement and achievement motives: Psychological and sociological approaches* (pp. 7–74). San Francisco: Freeman.

Spielberger, C. D., Gorsuch, R. L., & Lushene, R. E. (1970). *Manual for the State-Trait Anxiety Inventory.* Palo Alto, CA: Consulting Psychologists Press.

Stokols, D. (1972). On the distinction between density and crowding: Some implications for future research. *Psychological Review, 79,* 275–277.

Strickland, B. R. (1978). Internal-external expectancies and health-related behaviors. *Journal of Consulting and Clinical Psychology, 46,* 1192–1211.

Strickland, L. J., Lewicki, R. H., & Katz, A. M. (1966). Temporal orientation and perceived control as determinants of risk-taking. *Journal of Experimental Social Psychology, 2,* 142–151.

Strube, M. (1991). Unpublished data.

Suls, J. & Fletcher, B. (1985). The relative efficacy of avoidant and nonavoidant coping strategies: A meta-analysis. *Health Psychology, 4,* 249–288.

Swann, W. B., Jr., Stephenson, B., & Pittman, T. S. (1981). Curiosity and control: On the determinants of the search for social knowledge. *Journal of Personality and Social Psychology, 40,* 635–642.

Thompson, E. P. (1990). *Individual difference moderators of extrinsic reward effects: A person × situation approach to the study of intrinsic motivation processes.* Unpublished master's thesis, New York University, New York.

Thompson, S. C., Cheek, P. R., & Graham, M. A. (1987). The other side of perceived control: Disadvantages and negative effects. In S. Spacapan & S. Oskamp (Eds.), *The social psychology of health* (pp. 69–93). Newbury Park, CA: Sage.

Triplett, N. E. (1898). The dynamogenic factors in pacemaking and competition. *American Journal of Psychology, 9,* 507–533.

Wallston, K. A. & Wallston, B. S. (1981). Health locus of control scales. In H. M. Lefcourt (Ed.), *Research with the locus of control construct: Vol. 1. Assessment Methods* (pp. 189–243). New York: Academic.

Weiner, B. (1985a). "Spontaneous" causal thinking. *Psychological Bulletin, 97,* 74–84.

Weiner, B. (1985b). An attribution theory of achievement motivation and emotion. *Psychological Review, 92,* 548–573.

Weiner, B. & Kukla, A. (1970). An attributional analysis of achievement motivation. *Journal of Personality and Social Psychology, 15,* 1–20.

Weinstein, N. D. (1980). Unrealistic optimism about future life events. *Journal of Personality and Social Psychology, 39,* 806–820.

Weinstein, N. D. (1984). Why it won't happen to me: Perceptions of risk factors and illness susceptibility. *Health Psychology, 3,* 431–457.

Weinstein, N. D. (1987). Unrealistic optimism about susceptibility to health problems: Conclusions from a community-wide sample. *Journal of Behavioral Medicine, 10,* 481–500.

West, M. O. & Prinz, R. J. (1987). Parental alcoholism and childhood psychopathology. *Psychological Bulletin, 102,* 204–218.

White, R. (1959). Motivation reconsidered: The concept of competence. *Psychological Review, 66,* 297–330.

Williams, J. E., Watson, J. R., Walters, P. A., & Williams, J. G. (1983). Construct validity of transactional analysis ego states: Free child, adult, and critical parent. *Transactional Analysis Journal, 13,* 43–49.

Wolfe, R. N. & Kasmer, J. A. (1988). Type versus trait: Extraversion, impulsivity, sociability, and preferences for cooperative and competitive activities. *Journal of Personality and Social Psychology, 54,* 864–871.

Wolfgang, A. K. & Zenker, S. I. (1982). *Betting behavior as a function of sensation seeking and control motivation.* Paper presented at the annual meeting of the Eastern Psychological Association, Baltimore.

Wolfgang, A. K., Zenker, S. I., & Viscusi, T. (1984). Control motivation and the illusion of control in betting on dice. *Journal of Psychology, 116,* 67–72.

Wong, P. T. P. & Weiner, B. (1981). When people ask "why" questions, and the heuristics of attributional search. *Journal of Personality and Social Psychology, 40,* 650–663.

Woodward, N. J., & Wallston, B. S. (1987). Age and health care beliefs: Self-efficacy as a mediator of low desire for control. *Psychology and Aging, 2,* 3–8.

Woodward, N. J., Wallston, K. A., & Wallston, B. S. (1983). *Age related differences in desires and expectancies for control.* Paper presented at the annual meeting of the Southeastern Psychological Association, Atlanta.

Wortman, C. B. (1975). Some determinants of perceived control. *Journal of Personality and Social Psychology, 31,* 282–294.

Wortman, C. B. (1976). Causal attributions and personal control. In J. H. Harvey, W. J. Ickes, & R. F. Kidd (Eds.), *New directions in attribution research* (Vol. 1, pp. 23–52). Hillsdale, NJ: Erlbaum.

Wortman, C. B. & Brehm, J. W. (1975). Responses to uncontrollable outcomes: An integration of reactance theory and the learned helplessness model. In L. Berkowitz (Ed.), *Advances in experimental social psychology* (Vol. 8, pp. 277–336). New York: Academic.

Wright, L. (1988). The Type A behavior pattern and coronary artery disease: Quest for the active ingredients and the elusive mechanism. *American Psychologist, 43,* 2–14.

Zenker, S. I. & Berman, A. C. (1982). Performance estimates and causal attributions as a function of individual differences and situational variables. *Journal of Psychology, 111,* 91–95.

Zimmerman, M. A. (1990). Toward a theory of learned hopefulness: A structural model analysis of participation and empowerment. *Journal of Research in Personality, 24,* 71–86.

Zimmerman, M. A. & Rappaport, J. (1988). Citizen participation, perceived control, and psychological empowerment. *American Journal of Community Psychology, 16,* 725–750.

Zuckerman, M. (1979). *Sensation seeking: Beyond the optimal level of arousal.* Hillsdale, NJ: Erlbaum.

AUTHOR INDEX

SUBJECT INDEX

Academic achievement, 84–85, 89–93
Account episodes, 75
Achievement behavior, 34, 82–93
Achievement motivation, 5, 94–95
Adult children of alcoholics, 131, 175
Age differences, 30–34
Alcohol use, 134–135
Arousal level, 137
Aspiration level, 82–85
Attributional activity, 102–108
Attributional complexity, 104–105
Attributional style, 151–152
Attributions, 88–92, 101–118, 151–152
Anxiety, 120–125

Belief in a just world, 76

Cardiovascular problems, 24, 135–137
Challenges, response to, 85–87
Community involvement, 65–66
Competence motivation, 4
Conformity, 70–73
Contraception, 61–62
Coping strategies, 127–130
Counterattitudinal arguments, 68–70
Crowding, 77–78

Depression, 139–153
Desirability of Control Scale
    discriminant/convergent validity, 17–29
    factor analysis of scale, 16–17
    internal consistency, 13–15

Desirability of Control Scale (*cont.*)
    scale development, 12–13
    test–retest reliability, 15–16
Developmental issues, 174–178

Education level, 34
Edwards Personal Preference Schedule, 27–28
Effectance motivation, 4
Ethical behavior, 86–87
Extraversion–introversion, 28–29
Extrinsic motivation. *See* Intrinsic motivation
Extrinsic rewards, reaction to, 96–98

FIRO-B Scale, 25–26
Friends, 49, 53–60, 175–176

Gambling behavior, 155–169
Gender differences, 30–32, 178
General Causality Orientation Scale, 95–96

Health, 132–137
Helping behavior, 73–75
Hemispheric activation, 173
Hope, 126–127
Hypnotic susceptibility, 173–174

Illusion of control, 109–115, 156–162, 164–166, 168
Interaction style, 38–49
Intrinsic motivation, 5, 93–98

195